Uncommon Sense
for Parents with Teenagers

Uncommon
Sense
for Parents
with Teenagers

Michael Riera, Ph.D.

Celestial Arts
Berkeley, California

Celestial Arts
P.O. Box 7123
Berkeley, California 94707

Cover design by Fifth Street Design

Text design by Victor Ichioka

Library of Congress Cataloging-in-Publication Data

Riera, Michael.
   Uncommon sense for parents with teenagers / Michael Riera
       p.   cm.
   ISBN 0-89087-749-1
   1. Parent and teenager—United States.   I. Title.
HQ799.15.R54   1995
649'.125—dc 20   94-38317
                                                           CIP

First Printing, 1995

                5   6 / 00 99 98

To Betty and Pat Riera,
who made it all possible
for Peter, Tim, and me.
Love and thanks.

✤ CONTENTS ✤

❧ Parent Questions ❦

Commonly asked questions,
and where to find the responses:

❧ ACKNOWLEDGEMENTS ❦

Without the assistance of Megan Twadell-Riera and Joe DiPrisco this book would not have been written. Many, many times I've had to borrow Megan's confidence in me and my ideas. And without Joe's editing and continual questioning skills, the book would have been a shell of what you hold in your hands. I owe a great deal to both Megan and Joe. Thank you.

I also want to thank all of the readers who examined and commented on the manuscript in its various stages of completion— Carol Twadell, Julie Terraciano, Jane Dirkes, Al Hammer, Bodie Brizendine, John Dyckman, Hadley Hudson, Mario DiPrisco, Guy Stiles, John Erdman, and Lenzie Williams. Your input was essential.

My agent, Peter Beren, and all the people at Celestial Arts have been terrific. My deepest thanks to David Hinds, Veronica Randall, Colleen Paretty, Kathryn Horning, Fifth Street Design, and Victor Ichioka. You have made this first book a pleasure from start to finish.

Finally, I want to thank Celestial Arts for publishing this book and giving me the opportunity to thank a few of the people who have most shaped my thinking over the years: Peter Baldwin, Harry Kisker, John Dyckman (again), Robert Green, and Amadeo Giorgi. Thank you.

❧ PREFACE ❧

This text grew out of thirteen years of experience working with more than six thousand teenagers and more than two thousand parents in a variety of settings, from middle schools to colleges, from residential treatment programs to college preparatory schools.

For me, adolescence is a fascinating stage of life. I feel most optimistic when around teenagers. If this sounds strange, understand that I typically see their *best* aspects—the growing-up and reaching-out aspects—that are too infrequently seen at home. Adolescence is not a phase of life to be feared; rather, it is one of fascination, curiosity, and unexpected twists, and, as such, it is quite different from the previous stages of childhood.

What parents need is a translation of this period that makes sense and is useful. The isolation that parents of teenagers often feel is quite profound. You'll find lots of books on infancy and childhood, but few on adolescence. It is as if we hold our collective breaths from the end of childhood to early adulthood, and then breathe an enormous sigh of relief once adolescence has passed. I hope to replace the isolation, silence, and fear that accompany parenting during this period with optimism and hope. This book deals exclusively with the high school adolescent, grades nine through twelve, and conveys the range of viewpoints, struggles, and conclusions of the teenagers and parents who have come my way. While I have never heard the same conversation twice, all have carried an implicit desire for understanding that often forms the foundation of a solution.

This is not a how-to book because all teenagers are not the same. While it is true that they all, more or less, traverse the same terrain, it is equally true that they do so with different styles, idiosyncracies, and personalities. Just ask any parent who has more than one child. As you come to understand the context of the adolescent world, so will you recognize and admire the uniqueness of your child. Stereotypes of teenagers are misleading and can be blinding.

Mom: (*to her son walking in the door after baseball practice*) "So, how was school today? Anything interesting happen?"

Son: (*as he noses through the refrigerator*) "Nah, just a typical day. Is there any more orange juice?"

Mom: "Uh, no. We finished it this morning. So, nothing exciting in school today…oh, didn't you have that history test today? How do you think you did?"

Son: "Yeah, it was easy. Any soda in the garage?"

Mom: (*getting discouraged*) "No. Your father didn't do the shopping for this week yet…how about practice today? Was it a good practice?"

Son: (*as he heads towards his room with a bowl of cereal*) "The usual."

Mom: (*a bit exasperated*) "John, how come you don't talk to me anymore, let alone tell me what happens at school?"

Son: (*mildly surprised, but sort of smug*) "Geez, what is this Twenty Questions or something? I'm going to my room; call me when dinner is ready."

(*The son then proceeds to his room where he gets comfortable on his bed, eating his cereal, and listening to music—which, to his mother's ears, is rather loud and somewhat dissonant, and of course prompts her to request that he turn it down.*)

Mom: (*remembering to knock on the door*) "John. John, do you hear me?"

Son: (*waiting just a bit longer than necessary*) "What is it? What do you want now?"

Mom: (*opening the door and sticking her head into her son's room*) "John, please turn the music down. I'm trying to get some work done out here and I can't concentrate with that music so loud."

Son: (*with an exaggerated exhalation*) "OK, OK! I'll turn it down." (*Then, while taking his time and exaggerating his effort, he mumbles just barely loud enough for his mom to hear*) "Wouldn't want to do anything to help me relax now, would we?"

Mom: "Did you say something?"

Son: (*barely turning the music down*) "Nothing. There, it's turned down. Happy now?"

(*Mom walks away more perplexed and frustrated than before.*)

(*Five minutes later the music has miraculously gotten louder, or maybe it is just beginning to have a cumulative effect on Mom.*)

Mom: (*knocking on the door again, only slightly harder this time*) "John. John, turn the music down! (*Then after a moment of no response she opens the door.*) "John, *please* turn the music down."

Son: (*in a very irritated tone*) "Geez, don't you believe in knocking! I mean, don't I get any privacy? I don't just walk in on you and Dad, do I? How about giving me a little respect once in a while?"

Mom: (*at the end of her rope and quite exasperated*) "Just turn the music down!"

(*At this point World War III is imminent. When Mom does walk back down the hall she is shaking her head and wondering what has happened to her son. She also wonders what she did to deserve this, and furthermore, what she did to bring this about. Where, she asks herself, did she go wrong as a parent?*)

When this story is told to a group of teenagers, they immediately start laughing and nodding their heads, because they know this happens in their family as well as in most of their friends' homes. However, when the same story is told to parents, they first look nervously at the floor and only after a few moments do they begin to smile to themselves before looking around to see others smiling. We then begin to examine the story to understand the underlying rationale at work here along with alternative parent responses that avoid WWIII and the bad parenting/bad kid conclusions. You see, there is a kind of logic at work here, but teenagers can't articulate it in any consistent manner because they don't understand it themselves. In fact, once they understand it they are by definition no longer adolescents. Thus, parents have to uncover and translate this logic and learn to respond to their teenager on their own.

Parents and teenagers possess dissimilar world views that inform their behaviors, attitudes, and interpretations of events in very different ways. But teenagers don't want an adversarial relationship anymore than you. In fact, when talking about this book with several teenagers, they said, in effect, "If this book accomplishes nothing else other than helping parents to realize that we are not the enemy, it will have been worth the effort."

Ultimately, you are responsible for bringing up your child, and with this responsibility resting squarely on your shoulders, it makes sense to use a variety of resources: discussions with other parents, various articles and books (in addition to this one), reflection on your own adolescence, and professional consultations when appropriate. It is this responsibility that also makes you a critical and discerning consumer. Take the ideas that work immediately for you, modify others, and set the rest aside. But don't set anything aside until you've challenged yourself to understand why you are setting it aside; otherwise you'll be short-changing your developing understanding of your adolescent.

Parenting an adolescent is not an easy job. I am neither parent nor adolescent. However, I have a clear window into both their worlds. I've been surprised by parents' intense yearning for information, education, and ideas to help them understand a broad range of teenage behaviors. At the same time I've also noticed that the more general questions asked in a large group setting are often followed up with more intimate questions in the privacy of my office. This book is designed to address both sorts of questions. Sprinkled throughout the text are numerous individual stories, anecdotes, conversations, letters, and quotations from teenagers that illuminate the book's ideas.[1] These stories also tell the reader about what is happening in other parent-adolescent relationships.

This book is question-driven. After the first three chapters, which are overviews of the parent-adolescent relationship, the adolescent world, and high school, the book is a series of responses (not answers) to questions commonly asked by parents and other adults who work closely with adolescents. The Table of Contents reflects the general topics covered; the Table of Questions is a list of parents' questions addressed in the text. Remember, questions that you feel are not relevant to your situation may indeed hold the seeds to solutions for a host of other problems, which is why reading the entire text is important. You'll notice the questions are responded to in digressive and progressive ways that work together to develop the principles of a positive approach to the parent-adolescent relationship. While this book is not meant as a recipe book of solutions, reading others' successful resolutions will inspire and give you the confidence to design solutions appropriate to your life, your values, and your family. This does not happen overnight, but gradually over time. So, let's begin.

Endnote

1. The quotes from adolescents in this book are not direct quotations; instead they are samples of the kinds of things I have heard consistently during the past thirteen years. Also, all potentially revealing details were changed in the interests of confidentiality.

❧ CHAPTER 1 ❦

The Parent-Adolescent Relationship

Conventional wisdom has cast the parent-adolescent relationship as unavoidably adversarial. Both sides view the other as "the enemy"—a most unfortunate and destructive role in which to be a parent or an adolescent.

This book assumes that conventional wisdom is wrong. In fact, it suggests a very different and more useful picture of the parent-adolescent relationship. But first, where has this adversarial notion come from, and why has it gone unchallenged for so long?

On a typical evening when a group of parents gather to discuss and learn about adolescence, we start with two brainstorming questions. The first: "When you think of the generic teenager, what descriptive words come to mind?" This list, written on the left side of a blackboard, is generated quickly.

Then we move to the second question: "What are some of the daily choices as well as long-term decisions that adolescents face while in high school?" This list also comes easily, though generally not as quickly nor as playfully as the first, and it is written on the right side of the blackboard.

Take a minute to look at the two lists in Figure 1.

Figure 1

Words That Describe Teenagers	Issues and Decisions of Teenagers
Selfish, moody, idealistic, unpredictable, funny, lethargic, psychotic, irresponsible, surly, independent, angry, irritable, dependent, demanding, sullen, selectively responsible, manipulative, challenging, sulky, posturing, self-conscious, argumentative, disrespectful, stubborn, sneaky, scared, insecure, narcissistic, vulnerable, hungry, sleepy, and aloof.	Types of friends they want; kind of friend they want to be; sexual relations, sexuality, alcohol and drugs; importance of school and grades; class issues; economic worries; racism; existential identity; relationship to family; figuring out who they are and what they stand for; matching their insides with their self-perceived outsides; college; career; AIDS; daily violence around them; environmental concerns; ambiguity about all of the above.

Looking at these lists side-by-side, parents tend to have a number of reactions, best summed up as: "Anybody in that condition (words on the left) shouldn't be making those decisions (phrases on the right)." Then, parents are hit with a second, more powerful realization: teenagers *are* in this condition, they *are* facing these issues, and they *must be* making such decisions. As parents, you need to fully recognize this fact and reconsider your role as it relates to their struggles. This does not mean convincing your teenager to make decisions that are "right" by your standards, nor does it mean sitting by passively with your fingers crossed. It especially doesn't mean doing more of what got you through the previous thirteen years of your child's growth. Adolescence is an entirely different game, and the rules and goals have changed drastically. So drastically, in fact, that the old "tried-and-trues" often make things worse. We'll come back to this point in a moment.

When I engage teenagers in this same sort of brainstorming about their parents, the results are just as eye-opening. One set of questions is used to address three different periods in the parent-child relationship. The first time through, the questions are about an infant; the second time about a third grader; and the third time about a sophomore in high school. The questions are: "What does a typical parent want for their infant/child/adolescent? How do parents show this in their behaviors and attitudes toward their child?" See Figure 2 for their responses.

Figure 2

Infant	Third Grader	Sophomore
Lots of attention, encouragement, play, toys, affection, wanting to be with them, touching, singing, reading aloud, showing off, pride, excitement, providing for, pure joy, "can't get enough" of the infant, total acceptance	Involvement in their life, organizing their activities (dance, music, sports, etc.); encouragement and monitoring in school, teaching, helping with homework; giving responsibilities and overseeing them; gentle criticism; gentle feedback; limits and rules with limited freedom; teaching difference between right and wrong; appropriate expectations	Yelling, lots of guilt, excessive limits and rules, overcontrol, encouragement, choice, unrealistic expectations, support, nagging, punishment, limited praise, harsh criticism, overinterest in their life (excessive and obsessive), "little talks" and family dinners, "too much fun equals trouble," focus on their friends and types of people they are, judgmental jealousy, lack of meaningful contact, conflict, loud arguing, too many questions, no trust

Clearly, teenagers see their parents as helpful and caring through childhood, and as intrusive, mistrustful, and controlling in adolescence. Quite a shift of perspective! In fact, it is such a radical shift that teenagers can't even focus on what their parents want for them; they tend to focus exclusively on their parents' negative and restrictive behavior. However, with a little prodding, they can intellectually understand that their parents haven't deliberately chosen to switch from loving and caring to misunderstanding and nagging. They even get the idea that perhaps parents are not really sure how to go about this whole parenting thing with a teenager. Sure, they handled infancy and childhood without too many hitches, but that doesn't necessarily prepare an adult for adolescent parenting. When teenagers understand this, they also begin to see how they can help, even "coaching" their parents in a developing partnership. They have a lot of influence if they choose to make use of it—quite a mind-boggling concept to most fourteen-year-olds.

Take a moment now to look at both lists (Figures 1 & 2). At first, both seem to support the adversarial nature of the parent-adolescent relationship. Consider, however, what happens when your child starts high school. Until this point, you have acted as a "manager" in your child's life: arranging rides and doctors' appointments, planning outside or weekend activities, helping with and checking on homework. You stay closely informed about school life, and you are usually the first person your child seeks out with "big" questions. Suddenly, none of this is applicable. Without notification, and without consensus, you are fired from the role of manager. Now you must scramble and restrategize; if you are to have meaningful influence in your teenager's life through adolescence and beyond, then you must work your tail off to get rehired as consultant. And this is how it should be! Many of the adversarial aspects of the relationship stem from both parent and adolescent not understanding and appreciating this essential shift in roles.

Since parents have experienced only managerial roles in their child's life, they usually see no reason to change as the child enters adolescence. At a loss to explain their teenager's sudden shift in behavior, many parents take on the managerial role with even more gusto and fervor. This, in turn, is met with resentment and often disastrous results. Other parents have the opposite reaction, becoming passive and virtually abandoning any role with their teenager (no role equals minimal conflict), which also meets with unfortunate results.

From the other side of the relationship, as adolescents become clear that the parent-as-manager role is no longer useful, they focus on freeing themselves, without much consideration for alternative roles. They want more say in their lives and will go to great lengths to get it—even tolerating and rationalizing the guilt associated with upsetting and actively pushing their parents away. Thus, it is a pleasant surprise for most adolescents when they realize that if the role can shift from manager to consultant, they can have their cake and eat it too. That is, if their parents relinquish the role of manager, they can have increasing autonomy without abandonment; their parents can actually serve as very useful and important advisors. After all, who knows a teenager's history better than her parents? Who wants only the best for her? Who will consistently take risks for her? Who loves her and forgives her no matter how much she messes up? Who believes in her at least as much as she does? However, these attitude shifts are possible only if parents can assume the new, less-directive advisor role, and if adolescents can trust their parents in this role—a point we'll come back to throughout the text.

As a consultant, you offer advice and give input about decisions when you are asked. Otherwise, you'll lose your client. You don't garner the automatic praise and admiration that you did earlier. And, when your client (teenager) asks for advice, you need to make sure that she really wants it. Sometimes, more than anything else, she simply wants your reassurances that she'll figure it out herself. Sometimes she will temporarily lose belief in herself and ask to borrow your belief in her for a short while.

> It's kind of weird. A lot of times I ask my parents for ideas about what to do about a problem or situation, but then I get upset with them when they start offering me advice! I know they think I'm crazy when this happens. It's just that somehow I need to figure it out on my own, and while I want their help, I also don't want to be treated like a little kid.

Offering advice is not helpful when the real problem is the teenager's lost belief in herself. A rule of thumb is not to take your teenager's request for advice too literally until the third time. Nobody wants a consultant who tries to take the business over. What you are doing is *not* doing—you are waiting, but not abandoning. As a consultant, you must also save your "power plays" for health and safety issues; everything else is negotiable on some level. Skipping a biology class is definitely not on a par with driving a car after drinking alcohol. Finally, at this stage in your relationship, you are no longer the focus of your child's praise and admiration; rather, you are often the scapegoat for their confusion about what it is to be an adolescent. (See Figures 1 and 2 earlier in this section.) As a manager, you were quite content to take their feedback personally, as a reflection of you; as a consultant, you must learn to not take most of their feedback personally, since it is often more about them than about you.

When my son was seven I remember how much he used to just hang around me. He would wash the car with me, help me mow the lawn, and ride to the dump with me, insisting all along the way that we honk the horn and wave to his friends. He even persuaded my wife to get him the same kind of jeans that I wore around the house on weekends. I gotta tell you, it was terrific! Not only that, but he really listened to me, and I could answer the questions he asked. I even overheard him telling a friend that I was probably the smartest man alive! But when he became a teenager everything changed. He challenged me and argued with everything I said. He complained to my wife that he wanted different kinds of clothes: "You know, I'm not fifty years old! I don't want to look like Dad!" And he steadfastly refused to ride in the car with me unless I promised not to honk at his friends. Furthermore, whenever we drove by his friends, he would slump down low in his seat so they wouldn't see him riding with me! He even insisted that I drop him off at the corner for school in the morning, rather than take him all the way to the school where people might see us together. Talk about an ego blow. The only consolation was that I saw lots of other parents dropping their kids off at other corners near the school!

A manager-parent tries to ensure that his child makes the "best" decisions. A consultant-parent focuses on helping her teenager develop and exercise "decision-making muscles." The outcome is at times less important than the exercise and development of the muscle. Adolescence is, in part, an active training period en route to adulthood. (Of course, few teenagers would agree with this statement, unless they were in a very peaceful, trusting, and introspective mood, which is not all that available to most parents.) Thus, there is room for "bad" decisions that are really "good" decisions. Or, as Mark Twain once said, *"Good judgment comes from experience, and experience comes from bad judgment."*

Also, continuing the consultant model, the seemingly conflicting issues of asserting independence and behaving responsibly are actually two integral parts of the growing-up process. With this in mind, parents work to develop trust in their adolescents' growing judgment, who in turn work to keep their parents up-to-date on their developing responsibility skills. Kids see how their increased responsibility leads to greater independence; they realize they can directly influence the world around them. Parents see how increased independence fosters increased responsibility, which in turn fosters optimism and trust in the parent-adolescent relationship. Breeches of responsibility and independence are seen for what they are: missed opportunities not to be taken personally or to be construed as complete failure.

The consultant model also has the advantage of more successfully avoiding the two most common errors in parenting teenagers: treating them like children (over-parenting or over-managing), and treating them like adults (under-parenting or abandonment). The first is avoided by understanding that your new role involves much less doing; the second, by being present and actively listening in order to make the most of your "consultations." Or, as one high school student put it:

> Be encouraging and interested in your child. Although it's nice not to have nosey parents always pressuring me about what's going on at school, sometimes I feel ignored and neglected when they are indifferent to my daily life.

As a consultant, you willingly give up the illusion of power in favor of real influence. Clinging to pseudo-power over a teenager is what inadvertently leads him into accepting sneakiness and lying as viable strategies within the parent-adolescent relationship.

> Part of my problem is that my parents think they control me completely. I mean, they think I actually follow all of their ridiculous restrictions. They have such an inflated and unrealistic view of me that it is scary. I really wish they weren't so naive about my life; then, at least, we could discuss reality with each other instead of make-believe.

In the long run, the shift from manager to consultant is vital and essential for the parent-adolescent relationship. Throughout this book, the differences in these roles are highlighted. Again, the only exceptions to the consultant role are in situations of health and safety; of course, determining when health and safety are in danger is a matter of perspective, one that most adolescents and parents disagree on. This is also addressed throughout the book. Finally, with consultant-parenting I am not advocating laissez-faire parenting; quite the opposite, for consultant-parenting is often demanding and time-consuming. Here's the payoff, though: it is also much more rewarding for both adolescent and parent.

❧ CHAPTER 2 ❦

The Adolescent World

What is the world of today's adolescent, and do I stand a chance of understanding it?[*]

Let's begin with an example from a parent to keep in the background as this discussion unfolds. We'll come back to it at the conclusion of the chapter.

> Saturday afternoon, Sheila (a junior in high school) was moping around the house. I asked her if anything was wrong and got the usual indecipherable grunt. I let it go; I've learned over the last two years that pursuit in these kinds of situations often ends in conflict. Anyway, she got a bunch of phone calls that afternoon that seemed to worsen her mood. A bit later, when I was putting the cars in the garage, I asked her if she needed the car tonight (I wanted to know whether to leave it out or not). She turned on me and said harshly, "Dad, I don't know, just leave me alone!" Hmm, what line had I crossed this time? But, knowing my request was truly innocent, I got indignant and asked again, adding a snide comment about her first reaction. This time she simply screamed, "I don't know yet! Why should I have to know yet anyway? My life doesn't have to be planned down to the minute just so I don't inconvenience you! Just leave me alone!"

---

[*] This chapter serves as both an overview and a review to the chapters that follow. As an overview it offers a general framework for understanding and working with adolescents. As a review, it ties all the text questions together. Thus, this section can be read before or after the rest of the text, though preferably before *and* after.

Needless to say, dinner was rather tense. After about five minutes Sheila declared she wasn't hungry and was going to her room. Unfortunately my wife reacted before I could catch her. "You have to eat something. You can't just live on air!" Of course my daughter turned on my wife and launched into a tirade for several minutes—mostly incoherent stuff, but centered around our trying to run her life. Anyway, it wasn't a pleasant interaction.

Later that night my wife looked in on Sheila and she was in tears—curled up on the bed crying to herself. My wife got her to talk for a little while, but after a few minutes Sheila became quite frustrated and asked to be alone. Later, we invited her to watch TV with us, which she eventually did. But she never did tell us what was going on.

The next day she woke up early and went to volleyball practice, and when she returned she was in great spirits. She was like a different kid! When we asked her about the previous night, she looked confused for a second and then dismissed it with a wave of her hand.

What is going on here? How can we possibly understand this kind of behavior, let alone react to it? We'll come back to this at the end of the chapter, but just keep it in mind as you read on.

In many respects, teenagers appear to be more like adults than children, and often seem to inhabit a mature intellectual world. You must remember, however, that they are not adults. Adolescence contains aspects of both adult and child worlds, but is wholly neither. Writer and psychologist Theodore Lidz gives a well-rounded description of the adolescent stage of life:

[Adolescence] is a time of physical and emotional metamorphosis during which the youth feels estranged from the self the child had known. It is a time of seeking: a seeking inward to find who one is; a searching outward to locate one's place in life; a longing for another with whom to satisfy cravings for intimacy and fulfillment. It is a time of turbulent awakening to love and beauty but also of days darkened by loneliness and despair. It is a time of carefree wandering of the spirit through realms of fantasy and in pursuit of idealistic visions, but also of disillusionment and disgust with the world and the self. It can be a time of adventure with wonderful episodes of reckless folly but also of shame and regret that linger. The adolescent lives with a vibrant sensitivity that carries to ecstatic heights and lowers to almost untenable depths.[1]

The adolescent world is one of complex needs and perspectives. To understand it, one must first examine a variety of adolescent "horizons of meaning." These unavoidable changes, taken together, serve as the necessary context for making sense of teenage behaviors and attitudes. They also serve as a guide for parental intervention or non-intervention. For the sake of clarity, the discussion is organized around five horizons: physical and cognitive; social; friendship; personal identity; and family and life events. These horizons must compete with one another for attention, and often demand different actions or nonactions, which also are at odds with one another. So, while in the following discussion these horizons are examined one at a time, bear in mind that they are experienced simultaneously.

I. Physical and Cognitive

Before puberty, most children have established a fairly consistent and reliable manner of dealing with the world. However, with the onset of puberty and its incessant hormonal changes, this stability is lost. Adolescent girls are roughly two years ahead of boys in terms of physical maturity. Most girls have passed through the initial shocks of puberty by age thirteen, and age fifteen for boys. As an example of how these changes affect the child, boys typically double in strength from age twelve to age seventeen. Often, they literally don't know their own strength. In addition, a torrent of sexual feelings begin to emerge. These uncontrollable physical changes are definitely felt by the typical adolescent.

I was behind all my friends in terms of how fast we went through puberty—far behind. I still remember gym class in the ninth grade. During the winter we spent most of the time playing basketball, which is a sport I usually like. The problem was that we had to wear tank tops. I still didn't have any hair under my armpits, and I was afraid that someone might notice this and make fun of me. So I always kept my arms at my side, even though the gym teacher constantly yelled at me to raise my arms on defense. But there was no way I was going to lift my arms! I never even changed in the locker room with everybody else. I always got to class early so I could change before anyone else got there, and then I hung around late and got changed after everyone left. I never took a shower. It was definitely the worst part of freshman year for me.

Along with these physical changes is a profound shift in cognitive processes. Swiss psychologist Jean Piaget called this the move from *concrete operational thinking* to *formal operational thinking*. This shift can be compared to the difference between watching a movie on a four-inch black-and-white television and seeing the same movie in a state-of-the-art theater with surround-sound and interactive capabilities. Concrete operational thinking is limited to the present and to physical reality; formal operational thinking handles abstract concepts, ideas, and possibilities. This shift of thinking is obvious in the adolescent's sense of humor. Before puberty, most childrens' sense of humor is quite literal: when you say, "Look at the clock and tell me what time it is," your child might glance at the clock and playfully state, "What time it is." With adolescents, humor becomes somewhat more sophisticated—at least in the sense that they are not so literal-minded. Also, formal operational thinking opens the way for intellectual debate, conceptual thoughts, and reflective observation. It is a new way of experiencing the world that is quite exciting in its possibilities—and simultaneously overwhelming because of these possibilities.

This shift does not happen overnight. It typically begins around age eleven or twelve and becomes the dominant way of thinking around age fourteen. Thus, your teenager's inconsistent behaviors and attitudes are often the result of rapid switches between concrete and abstract thinking. These are the times when you can have an intellectually interesting and satisfying conversation with your daughter only to turn around and hear her whining like an eight-year-old about not wanting to eat her broccoli. Ninth-grade teachers see this process daily.

> I never had the words to put to this phenomena before understanding these oscillations between concrete and formal thinking. In ten years of teaching ninth grade English, I've seen a lot of inconsistencies that I intuitively knew the kids couldn't control, but I never knew why. At first I took it as a professional insult when students couldn't replicate their verbal insights about literature into equally insightful essays. Then I thought they were just lazy. But one day, after watching a particularly earnest student struggle painfully with an essay, I realized that he just couldn't do it, no matter how hard he tried! Since then I've learned to keep my tests and quizzes fairly concrete for the first part of freshman year, gradually making the shift to ideas and motives over the course of the year.

These frequent shifts between concrete and formal thinking can also help explain some of your adolescent's school difficulties. For instance, since all adolescents progress at somewhat different rates, a ninth-grade science class like biology that depends on a certain amount of abstract thinking will, theoretically, be within reach of the kids who have firmly established abstract thinking but be just out-of-reach of those who haven't yet fully made the shift. Thus, if your child experiences surprising difficulties in a class like this during the ninth grade, it often isn't just a matter of his not working hard enough or socializing too much with friends. Sometimes, his current stage of cognitive development is the problem.

Abstract thinking brings with it a new relationship to time. To a child, the future is very short-term. Children ask, "What's for dinner?" or "What's on TV tonight?" In this stage, the future is limited to concrete possibilities. Thus, a question like, "What do you want to be when you grow up?" can be answered. Adolescents, on the other hand, are more interested in the question, "What kind of person do you want to be when you grow up?" Adolescents who have firmly grasped abstract thinking can imagine the future in the present, reflect upon the past, and weigh the short-term losses and the long-term gains of certain decisions as they relate to an imagined future. They can also manipulate ideas in their heads without acting upon them physically. Before adolescence, action is thinking and thinking is action; during adolescence, thinking needs minimal action, because the thinker enters the realm of ideas and imagination. Thus, when adolescents sit in their rooms for several hours listening to music, seemingly lost to humanity, they might actually be using their new-found skills—which are not, unfortunately, as visible to parents as learning to ride a bicycle (recall the mother and son dialogue in the Preface).

This developing self-consciousness that comes with abstract thinking is both a blessing and a curse. The blessing is the ability to learn from events without painful repetition, that is, to extrapolate a lesson from a single instance and apply it to a multitude of similar cases. For example, once students stumble through the various unwritten social mores of high school, they learn these implicit norms of behavior in other settings without having to go through the entire process each time. The curse of self-consciousness is that it also becomes a tool for self-disparagement and guilt, some of which is necessary but much of which is excessive. This means that teenagers not only experience pain in the moment, but they can also re-experience pain for a long time afterwards. Even worse, they can re-experience neutral events from other perspectives that put their actions in the worst light. For instance, in replaying the events of a previous night's party, most adults remember the good and the bad parts, though they tend to give relative over-importance to the *faux pas*. Adolescents do the same thing, but in the extreme. After all, they are relatively inexperienced with self-consciousness. Thus, they tend to exaggerate the negative to the point of, at times, blinding themselves to the positive. These are the kinds of things they're thinking about when they sit in their rooms listening to music. A senior in high school, Nick Parker, summarized this nicely in an article for his school newspaper ("Devils' Advocate," University High School, San Francisco, CA):

> When I get home, I have had a full day of school, and usu-
> ally a lot has happened. I often sit around for a while, and

think about what has happened. I sit there and analyze everything I said and did. I try to figure out what I did wrong and what I did right. I try to discover more about the people I talked to that day. What did she mean by that? Did he know I was just kidding? Did I hit a sore spot, or was she just generally pissed off? These are just basic questions that go through my head. So much goes on in my head, and no stone is left unturned. That school day cannot be resolved until everything has been completely settled in my mind.

Basically, I cannot do any work until I have dealt with what has happened. Usually this means I have a late start on my work, thus putting me in a position where I have to skip a bit on my homework.

This is where stress comes in. Some people think that their homework MUST be done, and what they did in school that day shouldn't be dealt with until all their homework is done. When your personal thoughts have not been settled, work is probably the worst thing you can possibly do to relax; hence stress is created.

To sum up, this shift into abstract thinking, accompanied by a rush of hormonal changes, can (and often does) change a person overnight. Imagine waking up in a body that has new physical dimensions and new sexual desires, with a mind that conceptualizes the world in drastically new ways and that carries an overwhelming sense of confusion about all these feelings—all without prior warning! This is the world of the adolescent.

II. Social

The social horizon encompasses the social pulls and issues of the adolescent's public world: the people they hang out with, the events they frequent, and the behaviors they engage in or don't engage in.

In high school, the social world takes on a new meaning. For a few teenagers, it becomes the focus of their existence and their means of maintaining and gaining prestige. For others, it becomes the bane of their existence. But for the majority of teenagers, the social world is an intermittent focus in their high school years—and beyond.

In the years prior to high school, the social mandate is to "fit in." The goal of most kids this age is to feel comfortable with, and accepted by, a group of friends. However, in this group, they cannot usually "be themselves," but must instead abide by the group's unspoken rules.

> I was getting a slice of pizza, and ahead of me in line were three boys who were about thirteen years old. They all had on low-top black sneakers with white socks; knee-length, baggy black shorts, faded T-shirts (two white and one black), skateboards with lots of Day-Glo decals, and the same buzz cuts with slightly longer hair on top. Nothing unusual here, except that after a couple of minutes I noticed the faded writing on the back of one of the T-shirts: "Dare to be Unique!" That sums up early adolescence: dare to be unique, as long as you have two or three other people to do it with.

This horizon changes quite a bit in the high school years. Initially, it is important that teenagers have a group to hang out with. Minimally, this means that they have people to eat lunch with and people they speak to occasionally on the phone. Maximally, this means a set social life in which the established group they belong to makes decisions on parties, clothes, group members, etc. While most adolescents fit in between the extremes, some do not. For the teenagers who never find a group in which they feel reasonably secure, these years can be very, very painful. The horizon of the social life can consume them and they may neglect other areas. They either obsess on how to join a social group or decide they don't need a group, either way feeling the acute pain of loneliness and blaming themselves for their perceived failure to fit in. These are not joyful alternatives, especially in the context of developing self-consciousness.

The social world is also where race and ethnic issues begin to surface. In grammar school, kids make friends and spend time with peers regardless of race or economic status. Such differences have little meaning to children. This continues through most of middle school, but in high school teenagers begin to notice these differences and are affected by them.

Let's begin with race. Adolescents are wrestling with questions of personal identity (described in detail later in this chapter), and as they turn away from parents, some turn to their ethnic roots as a source of confirmation and information. For many, this is an eye-opening experience; a blinder is now peeled back as they start to understand their lives through their cultural roots. At the same time, ethnic differences begin to assert themselves in the selection—and exclusion—of peers and activities.

> In junior high, I, an African-American, hung out with a white guy and two Mexican guys. We were all best friends. We did all sorts of things together: ate lunch, hung out after school, played sports, and watched movies together. But when we got to high school, everything sort of changed without any of us talking about it. It just wasn't the thing to do anymore. We all made new friends and pretty much didn't spend time with each other anymore. I mean, we still say "hi" and play on some of the same teams and everything, but we're definitely not best friends anymore. It is kind of weird that way.

Such ethnic conformity, which is often the implicit norm in American high schools, simply reflects contemporary society. There are, however, some teenagers who perceive how race is affecting them and their choice of friends. These students are able to decide to make diversity a criteria in their selection.

> It really hit me in the cafeteria one day. I looked around and suddenly realized that all the blacks were in one corner, the Latinos in another, the Asians in another and the whites in yet another. It was like there were these invisible dividing lines running through the cafeteria! From that point on I decided to cross the line as much as possible. I don't want to limit my choices in friends that way.

While ethnic differences are obvious and yet still difficult to address, economic differences are even more elusive for teenagers. Part of the difficulty with both issues is that most teenagers are clear on their intellectual and idealistic stances about race and economics, but cannot reconcile this idealism with the reality of their personal, day-to-day lives. Nevertheless, both issues permeate adolescent culture.

> I don't remember money being a big deal at all in middle school, but in high school it sure is. Well, not the money itself, but what it allows you to do, and by that, who you are friends with. I don't hang around any of my middle school friends anymore, mainly because of money, though I'm pretty sure they don't know that. Actually I'm not really sure what they think. Once we got in high school they got into doing all these things that cost a lot of money: skiing on weekends, buying clothes at fancy stores, going to lots of movies, and buying the latest computer games. It was no big deal for them; they just sort of took it for granted. But it was a big deal for me; I can't afford to do any of those things on a regular basis. And when I do, I feel guilty asking my parents for the money because I can see how much it hurts them (whether they say yes or no). And I'm not old enough yet to get a job. So at first I just made up a lot of excuses as to why I couldn't do things with those friends— you know, like baby-sitting or visiting relatives, that kind of thing. Anyway, over time I found that I didn't have much to talk to them about, since we weren't doing the same things on weekends anymore. Then they stopped asking me to do things with them. I don't blame them. I mean, I said "no" practically every time. So now I still talk to them and things, but we're not really good friends anymore.

Then there is the subset of adolescents from divorced families who are in joint custody arrangements and constantly move between two very different economic (and sometimes ethnic) worlds.

> Moving between my parents' houses is really bizarre. Basically, my dad shafted my mom in the divorce. He has

this big, expensive house with just about everything you can imagine: a hot tub and pool, a housekeeper and gardener, and an amazing stereo and television system. I don't really know what he does other than run some sort of computer company. On the other hand, my mom works as a secretary (she never worked while they were married because he didn't want her to!). She lives in a third-story apartment with one-and-a-half bedrooms—guess which one is mine. It is culture shock every time I go from one house to another! I mean, in one house I have more than a hundred CDs, and in the other we don't even have a CD player. It really pisses me off. But I'm not sure who I'm more pissed at: my father for shafting my mother so badly, or my mother for letting him do that to her so easily.

Like ethnicity, economics is a means of asserting independence for some teenagers. For students who have jobs during high school, work is a means of taking control of their lives, because they now have money to spend as they choose.

The social group is also an important place for self-discovery; eventually teenagers will learn to step back from the group to make their own decisions and to begin taking conscious control of their lives. But they can only step back from the group *after* being a member of it. As adolescents begin asserting their independence from their parents, the "safe place" of the social group takes on more and more importance. This group gives them an initial place to break away to, rather than breaking away from the family and into an abyss. The importance and draw of the social group is most obvious when, for one reason or another, a parent disapproves of certain friends or groups of people. Articulating this disapproval to the teenager invites disaster, and not articulating this disapproval invites self-criticism.

I know Sean is a good kid. It's just that some of the people he hangs around with worry me. I don't imagine they are a very good influence on him. But whenever I mention this to him he gets very defensive and inevitably storms out of the room. I don't know what to do. Whenever I say anything we argue, but if I don't say anything I feel like a lousy parent.

As we'll see in more detail a bit later, directly voicing disapproval often pushes the adolescent closer to the disapproved-of friend. In these instances, maintaining the friendship is a means of asserting independence from parents. Unfortunately, it often precludes teenagers from making their own decisions about the friendship and acting accordingly. If parents can contain their anxiety about the friendship, they create the reflective space adolescents need to make their own decisions. This technique works for a range of subjects, as we'll see throughout the text. For example:

> After junior year, my daughter decided to go back East for a month to visit various relatives, especially her paternal grandmother. While she was making plans, I stressed how much her grandmother would appreciate a gift. It didn't have to be anything expensive, just something thoughtful. I even offered to help pay for it. Well, as the departure date approached and she procrastinated in her preparations, I got pretty anxious about this gift. I mean, this was my mother-in-law and my husband's relatives she was going to see! But whenever I came near the subject, Linda bristled. The day before she left, I couldn't take it anymore. I approached her, determined to ask directly about the gift. But before I could get it out, she pulled a lovely brooch from her bag and sincerely (and with a fair amount of pride) asked if I thought Grandmother would like it. Needless to say, when she asked what I wanted to talk about, I suddenly managed to "forget."

III. Friendship

While the horizon of friendship is an aspect of the previous section, it is also much more than the social world and thus deserves special attention. As adolescents grow older, intimate friendship becomes a more vital aspect of their lives.

Friendship is the secure environment in which teenagers can experiment with new behaviors and ways of being; they can learn about themselves through the feedback and reflected appraisals of trusted friends; they can learn how to accept their friends' flaws; they can discover the type of friend they are and the type of friends they want to have; and they can learn the important skills of friendship: support, vulnerability, empathy, honesty, trust, and responsibility. Adolescence, by nature, is a very self-centered time of life, and it is through friendship and concern for others' well-being that this focus on self is punctured—and supplemented with compassion and empathy.

The potential benefits of friendship for the adolescent are profound. The conclusion of recent phenomenological research on best friendships of eleven-year-old boys gives a glimpse of what is happening. From this research there are a couple of points worth highlighting. First, the boys felt unself-conscious with one another and were therefore more open to learning about themselves and the world around them.

> It's easy for me to try new things with Paul, because I know he won't make fun of me or laugh at me. So I do stuff with him that I would never do with other kids. He can even tell me things that are hard to hear, but that are true. Like once I was complaining about a grade I got in a class, and after awhile he just said, "Stop complaining so much. All you need to do is study harder." And he was right.

Second, the friendship taught them how to resolve interpersonal conflicts. They learned how to compromise and listen to others' views.

> Yeah, sometimes we disagree on things, but nothing very serious. Usually it's over something stupid. But once we talk about it we can each usually understand the other's point. Then we can put it behind us and forget about it.

These qualities of unself-conscious expression, giving and accepting feedback, taking personal responsibility and resolving conflicts are vital skills in successfully navigating the teenage years. All are potentially present in strong friendships. Close friendships take the pressure off the family, encouraging the adolescent to leave childhood behind and move gracefully into the adult world. It is inevitable that as children enter adolescence they turn towards friends and away from parents.

The overlap between the friendship and social horizons is also a breeding ground for peer pressure. Most adults fear that peer pressure will persuade their child to take dangerous risks. To understand why certain risky behaviors are worthwhile for adolescents takes a little digging on the part of parents. The main consequence of saying "no" to negative peer pressure is not just withstanding "the heat of the moment," as most adults think. Rather, it is coping with a sense of exclusion as others engage in the behavior and leave the adolescent increasingly alone. It is the loss of the shared experience. Further, the sense of exclusion remains whenever the group later recounts what happened. This feeling of loneliness then becomes pervasive, and carries an easy solution—go along with the crowd. Psychiatrist Harry Stack Sullivan called loneliness the single most important organizing factor of the adolescent and adult individual, and by this he meant that the fear of loneliness organized people to avoid it at almost any cost, as the following example illustrates.

> I used to not drink at parties. I don't even like the taste of alcohol, so it wasn't all that difficult. Besides, nobody really made a big deal about it. But then, over time, as my friends began to drink more, it got kind of boring. I couldn't relate to what they were doing and laughing about because I was still sober. For awhile I just left the parties early with no big fanfare. But more and more I would be left out of the second "party"—the blow-by-blow account of everything that had happened after I had left. All of a sudden I began to feel more apart from my friends. I was lonely, even though I had several "good" friends. Anyway, that's why I started drinking and continued to drink throughout most of last year. I wanted to belong again.

IV. Personal Identity

Amid this swirl of cognitive and physical changes, and along with the social and friendship issues, is perhaps the most consuming of all adolescent tasks: self-definition. They begin to define, to themselves and to the world, just who they are and what they stand for. Obviously this is a lifelong process, but few adolescents appreciate this timetable. Rather, they expect to answer the question, "Who am I?" with the black-and-white thinking of the past.

As teenagers discover who they are, parents can expect to witness lots of experimentation with roles. Initially this is a very external process. Clothes are the most obvious and simplest way to begin this role exploration. For instance, your daughter may suddenly dress herself only in black. Or, your son may insist upon a very particular type of jeans or shoes. Or, perhaps your daughter will dye her hair in a rather dramatic color or your son will pierce his ear. Most of these behaviors are part of the process of self-discovery, as well as of self-expression. None, in themselves, are to be feared. They are, however, attention-getters (and precursors to what is a more internal and subtle process as adolescents get older). Giving some curious attention to these actions can go a long way in understanding your teenager's world. At this point, negative or fearful attention probably only forces her hand into going further (this is similar to what happens when you criticize her friends). Your curiosity, which is inevitably tinged with skepticism, lets your daughter know that you've noticed and offers her the space to arrive at her own conclusions which, in most cases, will help move her along in the process of experimentation as she creates her sense of personal identity.

Along with visible external changes comes an even greater number of internal shifts. As teenagers experiment with different external roles, they must attempt to reconcile these roles with their internal states. For example, your son may choose to play the "jock" role for awhile. This helps direct him in dress, friends, activities, and attitude. But at some point he will do an internal check: "Is this me? Does this external image match what I am inside? Is there more to me than this image can contain?" Of course, these questions are part of an evolution that adults accept as lifelong. But to adolescents this process is new and they think they should be able to find ready answers.

> Summer was so terrific, and I had such high expectations
> for school, but so far this has been an awful year. Over the

summer I worked at a restaurant with mostly college students and hung out with them in cafés drinking coffee
between shifts. It was terrific. They really listened to me
and were interested in what I had to say. We talked about
life, relationships, politics, and important things. I felt so
mature, so in control of my life. But I've lost that since
school began. It's like nobody is interested. My parents treat
me like a little kid with all sorts of silly restrictions. My
friends just want to pick up right where sophomore year left
off. Everybody is in their own little world and I'm lost!
Worst of all, I either fall back into my old ways or I stay
home alone, miserably depressed. Actually, I'm depressed
either way! How come I can't be myself anymore? This
really sucks.

For most adolescents, this search for themselves is a relentless two-
steps-forward, one-step-backward process. And it is difficult for parents
to tell where their adolescent is at any given moment.

Personal identity also involves spiritual explorations and questions.
If raised in an organized religion, adolescents often begin questioning
their faith, perhaps even breaking with it. On the other hand, those who
are not raised within a religion may seek some sort of belief system,
both as a means of self-determination and as a source of solace in difficult times. Some teenagers will explore various modes of spirituality,
such as spirituality of nature, without embracing a formal religion. Still
others explore a spirituality of community—witness the Grateful Dead
phenomena. None of these are necessarily good or bad; often they are
simply changes, frequently in a different direction from the family. In
this sense, exploring and developing personal identity is a two-step
process, with the first step defining "who you are not" (which in most
cases is your parents), and then moving towards defining who and what
you are.

Another important aspect of personal identity is gender. As emerging research[2] is showing, boys and girls have quite different educational
experiences. Briefly, when boys and girls move from elementary to
middle school, both experience a drop in self-esteem; however, girls

experience a disproportionately larger drop that stays constant throughout high school. This is alarming. While the solutions are not easy, there are some things that parents can do. First, it is important to maintain the same expectations for girls and boys, especially in the kinds of careers they choose. In this arena teachers must also maintain the same expectations for both sexes, and they need to encourage and insist that girls stay actively involved in class discussions, which, without attention and consistent invitation, often decreases over the four years of high school.

> It's really kind of strange. I [senior girl] remember that during freshman and sophomore years classmates always used to kid me about talking so much in class. I had an opinion about everything and wasn't shy about letting people know it. I even used to disagree and argue with my teachers during class, and I was often right! But during junior year, I somehow got timid, and started speaking less and less. Now [senior year] I hardly talk at all—I'm so afraid of saying the wrong thing and making a fool of myself. It's just easier to stay in the background and listen to what everybody else says—they all seem so sure of themselves.

Second, it is essential for girls to have female role models who are successful across a variety of professions. Boys and girls develop differently and, as a result, girls need female models of success, rather than trying to succeed through the male process of success.

High school is also a time when adolescents are beginning to wrestle with their value systems, needing to try out a variety of approaches rather than accepting their parents' verbalized values. While necessarily drifting from parents' values, teenagers are simultaneously noticing the differences in what their parents say and do. And when push comes to shove, they will point this out to you—usually without much tact. Teenagers are very observant, and they now trust their eyes more than their ears. What you do affects your kid's values more than what you say.

> I know I'm supposed to tell the truth and face the consequences and everything. But it's not like my parents are any

more responsible than I am. They're pretty hypocritical, which really pisses me off!...Like they're constantly on me to tell them exactly what time I'll be home. They even hold me to the minute! But when they have to pick me up or take me somewhere they are never on time. Just the other day I asked my mother to give me a ride to meet a friend at a movie theater, and she said fine. Well, when it was time to leave she was on the phone and even though I told her we had to leave, she kept on talking. Of course I got there late and didn't get to sit with my friend—we didn't even see each other until the lights went on when the movie was over! My mother couldn't understand why I was so upset. She said she was sorry, but then she expected everything to be fine, like it hadn't been a problem at all!

So does this mean you have to be perfect? Not at all. It does, however, imply that you are responsible for yourself. Adolescents don't need perfect parents; in fact, they are probably better off with less-than-perfect parents (who are more reflective of the real world). But they do need parents who acknowledge their own faults and shortcomings as well as their values and strengths. This parental responsibility creates space for the adolescent. When parents don't accept responsibility for their own actions, the teenager gets stuck with the blame. And nobody holds onto blame gracefully, especially when it isn't rightfully theirs. Thus adolescents begin, subtly, to learn various attitudes of irresponsibility. They become pseudo-responsible: they learn how to justify themselves, how to avoid acknowledging fault, and how to place blame on others, both appropriately and inappropriately. However, when parents accept responsibility for themselves and their actions, adolescents have room to be more honest with themselves. They learn to first acknowledge their own faults, which in turn allows them to improve on themselves, and ultimately to define themselves as well as feel more in charge of their lives. This is essential to developing a strong and secure personal identity. However, this is not an overnight process. Developing responsibility takes time and a fair amount of trial and error. (See Chapter 6 for more on this topic.)

V. Family and Life Events

Teenagers' relationships to various members of their family are a significant backdrop to all that they do. This backdrop includes family history, expectations (both explicit and implicit), and family composition.

Significant events in a family's history, such as divorce, death, a prolonged illness, or economic crisis, shape many of an adolescent's decisions, choices, and attitudes. If the event happened prior to adolescence, issues related to it will very likely resurface, usually during times of stress. I remember well one student who used to come by my office just prior to exams, at the end of first and second semesters. Her first visit was before first semester exams in her sophomore year and her last was just before graduation. She usually came by for one or two meetings at a time. Beginning with the first visit, and with all subsequent visits, she talked exclusively about her parents' divorce when she was eight years old. She never mentioned anything about exams. And with each meeting she picked up exactly where she had left off—whether it had been a week or four months since the last visit! In this manner she reinterpreted the experience of the divorce as an adolescent. That is, with her more developed thinking and relationship skills, she needed to and did develop a more complex and thorough understanding of the divorce and its effects on her.

All of us have what I call "stress buffer zones." Under ordinary circumstances we can tolerate added levels of stress without significant ramifications. But when, because of past or current traumas, the stress buffer zone is partially used up, teenagers are quite vulnerable to both new and old stresses. (See Diagram 1.) Adolescents are most susceptible at fairly predictable times: exams, proms, beginnings and endings of romances, anniversaries of traumatic events, and holidays, to name a few.

Diagram 1: Stress Buffer Zone

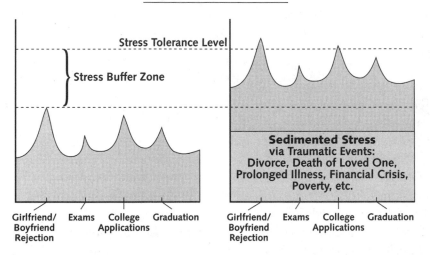

These are the times when an old event is most likely to come up for re-examination, both consciously and unconsciously. If it surfaces consciously, the teenager might talk or write about the event, ask questions for clarification, or reflect on the event in introspective moods. If the event surfaces unconsciously, the adolescent might show unwarranted moodiness, "act out" negatively, or make sudden significant changes in eating or sleeping patterns. We'll come back to some of these events and how adolescents deal with them later in the text; for now, suffice to say that teenagers see the world differently than they did as children and it is only natural and healthy that they reexplore significant events from the past.

Back to family relationships: in the early adolescent's world, parental expectations set the standard for pleasing or "good enough" behaviors. These include the areas of grades, looks, extracurricular activities, habits, friends, etc. These expectations become clear to the teenager in primarily two ways. The first is in explicit priorities stated by parents: attitudes like working hard, being honest, telling the truth, getting good grades, living a balanced life, and taking responsibility for one's actions. The second is implicit, learned by watching what parents (and other family members) do regardless of what they say. These realizations are confusing, but necessary, for the adolescent. (Recall the

"Friendship" section.) They begin to see their parents as real people—complete with human foibles, inconsistencies, and bad habits. This realization is at first terrifying. Suddenly, the people who several years earlier seemed omnipotent are exposed as really no different from the rest of the adult world—or from the teenager, except that they are older and more experienced.

> It's really weird. When I was a little kid I wanted to be just like my dad; I thought he was perfect. But then one day reality hit like a sledgehammer. We were at the hardware store together and when we went to pay the cashier, she overcharged him. He said something, and she got all upset and acted like a jerk. She even called him an asshole under her breath. But instead of standing up to her, he just said, "forget it" and paid the overcharge! On top of that, he apologized on the way out! I couldn't believe it—he had wimped out. It completely blew my mind, and I was pissed for quite awhile. When he asked me what was wrong I couldn't say anything. I mean, what am I going to say—no, nothing's wrong with me, Dad, the problem is that you're a wimp? That was probably the worst part. He didn't even get it.

Now, for the first time, many adolescents feel truly alone, and may for a brief while turn on their parents in angry rejection for being human. They are scared and vulnerable. And if vulnerability isn't safe, anger is the easiest alternative. In anger, one is active and seemingly in charge, instead of being in the more passive and potentially humiliating state of vulnerability. And teenagers, more than any other age group, will go to extremes to avoid humility and vulnerability.

If parents can accept this fall from grace as inevitable rather than a personal attack, then they can learn a great deal about themselves. After all, some of this adolescent feedback hits the bull's eye. It is also a clear sign that the parent-adolescent relationship needs to become more consultant and less managerial. If this shift can happen, family relations become fertile ground for the teenager to learn compassion and acceptance.

While many of these contradictions in parent's behavior are fully human and fairly harmless, some are quite damaging, mainly because they inadvertently reinforce adolescents' negative beliefs about themselves.

> Well, you know how hyper-conscious I am of my weight. And I was getting much better lately about not picking myself apart. That is, until last night. Sometimes I just can't believe that my parents are either so stupid or so mean. I took a break from studying at around 9:00 and went downstairs for a snack. There wasn't much, but there was some ice cream in the freezer. So I made a small bowl for myself. It was really not that much. As I was walking up the stairs I passed my father, who eyed the ice cream, looked at me, and again looked at the ice cream. Then he said, "Are you sure you want to be eating that? If you're not careful, the fat will sneak up on you!" He said it in a joking way, but it felt like criticism. I just gritted my teeth and went to my room. A little later I snuck down and finished all the ice cream, just to spite him! But ever since then I've had a guilt hangover. There is no way I can win. And I'm right back to thinking I'm fat again.

Family composition also plays a vital role in how teenagers perceive themselves and how parents perceive them. The eldest child tends to be the trailblazer in the family. Thus, the eldest child and the parents enter the uncharted territory of adolescence together. With the next child, parents believe, often erroneously, that what worked with the first child will work again. Younger kids have the advantage and the disadvantage of entering chartered territory with parents. At least parents have an idea of what to expect; on the other hand, they may be blind to essential differences between children. Also, if the eldest child was very successful (or very unsuccessful) at living up to the parent's expectations, the younger child feels pressure to do the same: Do I attempt to outdo my older sibling? Do I not even attempt that set of expectations and instead carve out my own niche? Or do I play it safe and stay average: "Nothing ventured, nothing lost?"

It's very frustrating. My older sister was a real sneak. She got in all sorts of trouble. By the time she graduated she had been caught skipping school too many times to count, had been caught stealing an exam, and had gotten arrested for drinking and driving! But the problem is, I'm nothing like her—and my parents refuse to see that. They are watching me and waiting for me to screw up. When I try to talk to them about this, the only answer I get is that they're not making the same mistake twice. I wish they could see that I'm a pretty good kid and deserve a little trust. I don't stand a chance until I get out of this place.

Or,

My sister and brother were real stars in high school: she was an All-State soccer player and he was valdectorian of his class. But I'm not like either one of them. I'm average at both sports and school, and that's fine with me. Really! I'm much more focused on people. In fact, all of my friends turn to me for help with their problems. Even though I'm a Peer Counselor for the school, my parents don't seem to notice. They're just always on me to get better grades and to do better in sports. Ninety percent of our fights have to do with them pushing sports and academics down my throat.

Then there are the only children who frequently carry the attention of the entire family's expectations. Because they can't see how siblings are treated, they frequently personalize non-personal events.

I love my parents and everything—it's just that sometimes it's too intense with just the three of us. It's like they notice everything about me! And if something goes wrong for me or we have a fight it's like a national disaster. Like when I didn't get a role in the school play they treated me like they expected me to have a nervous breakdown or something! I mean I was disappointed, but not nearly as much as they were. It was so weird that for awhile I thought something was really wrong with me for not feeling worse about not getting a part! Sometimes I wish they had had another kid; it would take a lot of the pressure off me. But then again, when I'm in the right mood, I like all their attention.

Finally, in any family, there is always the dynamic created when the last child leaves home. Aside from what the adolescent goes through (discussed later in the book) this change deeply affects all parents. Now, after raising children for the past 18 to 30 years, they must again focus on their relationship with one another.

> My parents have been a little edgy with each other lately, and I think some of it has to do with me going to college next year. I'm the youngest, so after I leave it's just the two of them. They've focused so much energy on me and my two brothers that I think they're a little unsure of what to do with all that energy once I leave. I know they still care for and enjoy each other, but still, some things are going to change.

And,

> Going away to college is going to be tough on my mom. I'm a little worried about her. Ever since my dad left [ten years ago] it has just been the two of us. She's been great, but she's been so obsessed with what's best for me that I'm not sure she'll know what's best for her once I leave. I know she hates her job—the only reason she keeps it is so that we can live in this big apartment and so I can go to private school. So I'm not sure what she'll do when she has the freedom to quit and start another career. Also, we've been like best buddies the last couple of years, and I'm worried that she doesn't have many friends to talk to once I leave.

Ideally, the family is the tap root that supports the adolescent through the winds, breezes, and periodic gales of adolescence. A strong and acknowledged parental commitment to their adolescent along with the determination to let her grow into her own person is what every teenager needs.

My parents were great throughout high school. They always let me know that they love me, even when I was being impossible. They were also always willing to hear the truth about my life, even if they didn't agree with what I was doing. We talked openly about tough issues like alcohol and sex, and they weren't afraid to let me know exactly what they thought, though they gave me the room to make my own mistakes. But when things were the worst with friends, boys, and school—I knew I could always count on my parents, even if they disagreed with how I was handling the situation.

There may be times when you don't believe it, but you and your feelings about your teenager are very important to her, as the following counselor's story illustrates.

Recently I was facilitating a retreat for the incoming senior class of a local high school. One of the exercises was about prioritizing commitments. At the conclusion of the exercise, which included a fair amount of writing and discussion, some seniors volunteered to go to the front of the room and state their most important commitment for their senior year. It was amazing to me, but more than sixty percent talked about family and parents. And most of them began with, "I'm sure my parents would be shocked to hear this, but..."

The Logic of Adolescence

At this point, each horizon has been illustrated with examples of its influence on adolescent behavior. But clearly, the horizons are not distinct; each overlaps and competes with another. Thus, adolescent decisions are not always what they appear to be. A teenager may make a decision out of free will and then change his mind when he discovers he is doing what his parents prefer. Thus, he may do the opposite of what he wants simply to assert his independence from his parents. Unfortunately, he buys this sense of independence at a high price, unwittingly giving up the confidence and personal power that come with making the choice *he* wants. It gets complicated quickly.

Let's ground all this in concrete terms by returning to the example at the outset of this chapter. What could have made Sheila, the moody adolescent, act the way she did from Saturday afternoon to Sunday morning? Several explanations may apply. From a social perspective, she may have been worried about being included with her friends in their Saturday evening plans. Thus, she was anxiously waiting for the phone invitation and couldn't offer a simple yes or no response to her dad's question about the car. To answer him would mean exposing her social vulnerability to her dad at a time when it was causing her a great deal of anxiety. And since for most adolescents it is easier to be angry than vulnerable, Sheila simply directed her anxiety back at her father (and later her mother) in the form of anger. But why the sudden mood change on Sunday? Perhaps at soccer practice she learned that all the plans fell through and everyone stayed home for the evening; so she wasn't left out after all.

From a romantic perspective, perhaps Sheila had said "no" to her friends in order to leave the door open to say "yes" to a guy she hoped would call and ask her out. Or, maybe she left the door open to phone the guy herself and ask him out, or at least talk on the phone for awhile. Thus, her angry responses to her parents might stem from her doubt and the tenuousness of her plans. She could end up empty-handed—home with her parents on a Saturday night. And what about the change on Sunday morning? After not hearing from the guy on Saturday evening, she may have heard from her friends (who also play on the soccer team and who saw the guy in question at a party the night before) how he had asked them all about Sheila and had really hoped she would be at the party with them.

From a sexual perspective (addressed more fully in Chapter 9), perhaps Sheila had had sex several weeks ago and on Saturday was over a week late with her period. She would then be extremely anxious and wouldn't know where to turn: to her parents, to the guy involved, to her friends, or to Planned Parenthood on her own? Should she go out or not? And Sunday—well, she got her period at soccer practice.

From a family perspective, perhaps her friends were planning on doing something that Sheila wasn't ready for—drugs, drinking, or older guys—and she resented her parents for her doubt and misgivings about going out with her friends. And possibly the next day at soccer practice she learned that the plans had fallen through miserably or that they were botched and everyone had gotten in big trouble. Either way, she felt good on Sunday about her decision to stay home.

Brainstorming numerous explanations like this shows that all are quite logical. I suggest coming up with four or five viable explanations about your adolescent's behavior before settling on any one, and in truth you won't know which (if any) is accurate until some time in the future. The point is that these possibilities afford you the explanations that adolescents can't yet offer. In turn, the explanations help you handle your anxiety while giving your adolescent the space to work through her anxiety. Or as Ben Furman and Tapani Ahola say in *Solution Talk: Hosting Therapeutic Conversations*, "Uncommon, imaginative explanations are often excellent catalysts for finding solutions."

In Closing

At the conclusion of one of my recent day-long workshops on the nature of adolescence, one of the participants, a very experienced and respected teacher, approached me. He said that he was now more amazed than ever that, given what is happening in teenagers' lives, they learn any math in his class! It is indeed quite a feat. Or as the writer and poet John Ciardi said: "You don't have to suffer to be a poet. Adolescence is enough suffering for anyone."

As we've seen so far, adolescence, at least in this country, is a pre-ordained existential crisis. It is the first such crisis of their lives; they are unable to put it into the perspective that experience affords. Adults who have that perspective tend to underestimate the impact of various events on teenagers' lives. Flunking a test and getting dumped by a boyfriend or girlfriend within a couple of days is analogous to an adult's losing a job and a spouse in the same time period. While "first loves" are a romantic memory from an adult perspective, they are a traumatic and angst-ridden experience for the adolescent. Remember that adolescence is the process of coming into one's own, but it is by no means a graceful unfolding. It is more like wrestling into one's own. Or as Bob Dylan said in "Like A Rolling Stone":

> *How does it feel?*
> *How does it feel?*
> *To be on your own.*
> *Like a complete unknown.*
> *With no direction home.*
> *Like a rolling stone.*

Many teenagers feel as if they are juggling two lives simultaneously: the leftover kid's and the emerging adult's. Or, as one student put it: "I've been under the influence of confusion ever since I entered high school! When will it stop?" With the development of self-consciousness and the resulting fear of humiliation, think about how to allow teenagers the graceful way out of situations. This is one of the hidden intentions of this book—to help you, the parent, help your teenager develop and maintain grace in a most awkward time of life.

Now, let's turn our attention to some of the questions asked most frequently by parents. The first deals with high school.

Endnotes

1. Lidz, Theodore, *The Person: His Development Throughout the Life Cycle*, pp. 298-299.

2. Greenberg-Lake: The Analysis Group, Inc., *"Shortchanging Girls, Shortchanging America."*

❧ CHAPTER 3 ❦

The High School Experience

Is there a pattern of experiences common to all kids during the four years of high school?

No! But there are some predictable issues that must be addressed during high school, though each adolescent navigates these issues in different ways and at different times. What follows is a rough sketch of high school year by year—but as always, the only thing that you can count on is that your teenager won't follow the pattern exactly.

Ninth Grade

This year begins with the transition from the known world of eighth grade to the unknown world of high school, to be revisited again in the transition from high school to college or work. In eighth grade, the adolescent was part of the oldest group of kids in the school. They were familiar with the terrain of the school, knew the faces of their classmates, understood the unspoken rules of the school, and were looked up to by the kids in the lower grades. In ninth grade, the typical teenager is met with a sea of change: an unfamiliar campus, many new faces, a vague understanding of the explicit rules of the school (never mind the implicit ones), and the stress of occupying the lowest rung on the seniority ladder—they are freshmen.

Socially, this means the adolescent must get to know and become established with a new group of people. Finding a social niche that includes a safe group to eat lunch with is typically high on the priority list.

By far the worst part of the day during freshman year was lunch. I never knew who I was going to eat with. I didn't have any one set of friends, so I had to decide every day where to eat and who to eat with. Of course, my biggest fear was that I would have to eat alone, which would have been the absolute worst. Honestly, I would start worrying about this at about 10:00 every morning! For awhile I even gave up lunch and just went to the gym to play basketball, but I got too hungry afterwards, so that didn't last.

Once ninth graders have found a place to fit in, they begin to search for the place where they can fit in as themselves, a long process that often includes moving away from their initial social group.

In ninth grade there is often a real split between boys and girls. The girls often receive a warmer reception and earlier acceptance into the school, especially by the junior and senior boys. In contrast, because of their lack of physical maturation, ninth grade boys often stand out compared to the older boys. This can also play out socially in terms of who gets invited to parties and who doesn't. Either way, at this point, both boys and girls come face-to-face with qualitatively and quantitatively different social and party scenes than they experienced in middle school. The choices are much more varied and the options are much more viable.

High school is so different from middle school. It's like two different worlds. All of a sudden I know kids who drive, there are lots of parties with alcohol and drugs, and some kids seem to stay out all night. Everything just seems so much faster and more exciting, but it can be a little over-whelming too.

This increased pace and availability is true throughout high school and college, and most students will confront these issues somewhere along the line. (See Chapter 7 for more on this topic.)

Entering high school also coincides with heightened sexual energy and awareness. Teenagers become attuned to the "group mind" of what the norms and expectations of high school are; to be sure, this "group mind" is not the accumulated wisdom of the ages, but the grandiose stories and exaggerations of the typical American high school.

> From freshmen year on, you get the feeling that everybody has more sexual experience than you. From the first day I felt behind. And sometimes there was this urgent sense to just have sex to get it over with—to be caught up with everyone else. But one night I stayed up late talking with a couple of friends and we talked honestly about sex (I guess because it was so late and we were all a little punchy). It was shocking! I was sure that they were both much more experienced than me, but it turned out that I was actually more experienced than either of them. Then we talked about how none of us had ever lied about what we had done—but then again we never corrected mistaken assumptions either!

Teenagers are also acknowledging and developing a relationship with their sexuality, which continues well beyond high school. However, if your adolescent is one of the roughly five to ten percent of the population that is gay, you can expect this aspect of his or her life to dominate others for a considerable period of time because of the internal and external conflict this lifestyle still generates in American culture. (See Chapter 10 for more on this topic.)

With their rapid physical changes, new sexual energy, developing self-consciousness, and the need to find a social niche, it is no wonder that the typical ninth grader is quite self-absorbed. This is perfectly normal, if occasionally disconcerting.

> I took my daughter out to dinner the other night to spend some one-on-one time together. I had been in and out of town on business for the past few weeks and hadn't spent any time with her. Well, the dinner was fine and our conversation seemed to flow quite smoothly. She was even listening to what I had to say. But after awhile I couldn't help noticing how she kept glancing over my shoulder every few minutes for a few seconds at a time. Later, when she went to the bathroom, I looked behind me, fully expecting to see

a school chum or perhaps a very attractive man. To my surprise I saw a giant, wall-mounted mirror! She had been looking at herself!

The move from middle to high school also means a significant shift in academic expectations. Students face an increased workload and degree of difficulty. Teenagers have to figure out where they fit in academically, given the number of new classmates they have encountered.

All through junior high I got mostly A's and a few B's without ever having to try too hard. But in high school I've been working much harder and only getting B's and C's. Everyone around me seems so much smarter than I'm used to, and lots of the kids are ahead of me in terms of what they already know, depending on which junior high they came from. Also, the teachers expect a lot more.

Then, new teaching methods and a different academic culture may require adolescents to relearn how to learn. With math, for example, a focus on small group work and portfolio assessments is jarring for some incoming students unfamiliar with these methods. They may expect the teacher to lecture and give tests in the traditional manner, and they find they must adjust, as do many parents, who often don't know about or understand these new methods.

High school math is so different from middle school. In eighth grade, my math teacher stood in front of the room and lectured for most of the period. Then we did some of our homework and he answered questions. In high school, my teacher hardly ever lectures. We mostly work in small groups and she just moves from group to group. And worst of all, we have to write out explanations of what we're doing. It isn't just numbers anymore!

Thus, a large part of freshman year is spent leveling the playing field. Students are getting caught up to one another in terms of the facts they know while also filling in the gaps around basic study skills and what it takes to be a successful student in high school.

For the first time in my life I have to really study. I can't do my homework in front of the TV anymore! Now I sit at a desk in quiet. I'm also having to think and understand instead of just memorize. Sometimes it's a real drag. Sometimes I even get headaches.

Most significantly, students are beginning to wrestle with attitude and priority shifts. They have to decide how important academics are to them. Academic success demands greater effort, so students must decide if they are willing to meet those demands or if they are going to sacrifice academic achievement in favor of the other aspects of their lives which are also placing higher demands on them than ever before.

Sometimes it feels like too much: all my teachers give more homework than I've ever had before; my basketball team practices more often and much harder; and I'm on the phone more than ever. I don't know what is most important anymore.

Finally, things are changing at a faster rate than ever at home, specifically in relationship to parents. Adolescents are now wanting more say over their lives and less say from their parents. This is rarely a graceful process. It is usually awkward, with the teenager only able to voice what he doesn't want, not what he does want. We'll cover this more completely in the sophomore year, when such behavior is most evident. But for now, during your teenager's freshman year, he'll probably still tell you that he loves you.

Tenth Grade

With the first year of high school under the belt, sophomore year provides a welcome relief. Tenth graders now understand more or less how the school works and where they fit in, both academically and socially. The boys' physical maturation is catching up to the girls'. Both sexes are either having more success in extracurricular activities and sports, or are slowly coming to grips with reality—no, they realize, they won't be the next basketball or tennis superstar. They are also seeking reassurance in, and control of, their bodies. This can mean weight lifting (and in the extreme, steroids) for the boys and food consciousness (and in the extreme, eating disorders) for the girls. (Many girls flirt with eating modifications at this point, most notably through dieting and exercise—see Chapter 15 for more on this topic.)

After finding a group to spend time with during the ninth grade, many teenagers begin to reassess their friendships as well as what they are looking for in friends during the tenth grade. Many yearn for closer friendships, in which they can be honest with feelings, ideas, and opinions—where trust and faith are the dominant values. With abstract thinking skills in place, teenagers construe these friendships in fairly idealistic terms. Past and current friendships are reexamined with this perspective. Few are able to withstand the scrutiny. Fortunately, many friends seem to undergo this process at roughly the same time, so with persistence and negotiation, deeper friendships are forged.

> I have basically the same friends that I had last year, but it is different. It's hard to explain. One-on-one conversations are deeper. In the larger group things haven't changed all that much. It's like we all have two different personalities—one in the group and one away from it.

Sometimes, however, groups of friends desire different kinds of friendship at different rates, in which case it is typical to see old friendship groups break up in favor of smaller and more diverse friendships. Either way, the friendship groups of ninth graders undergo significant pressure and typically change in the sophomore year. Often they continue changing well into junior year.

> When I look back at the beginning of freshman year, it is pretty embarrassing. I was so naive! I have new and better friends now who I hadn't even met then. I still talk with some of my old friends, but it all seems so superficial. I guess we all changed in different directions. It's not like anything bad happened; we just changed.

Or,

I thought I had good friends at the beginning of last [freshman] year, but they've done some things that I don't agree with, so I don't spend much time with them anymore. They were really mean to some kids that wanted to hang out with us—acting nice to their faces but laughing behind their backs. It was awful! I still spent time with them until I found some new friends, but I couldn't wait to get away from them.

At home, relationships are changing at a dramatic rate for most tenth graders (and their parents). Many experience home—more specifically, the privacy of their own rooms—as their only safe haven. Otherwise, home is a fairly volatile place. (Recall the mother and son dialogue where, in the end, both feel bad about the interchange, but neither knows how to go about changing the pattern which has developed.)

A major part of the problem is timing and expectations. When teenagers come home from school they often need to "detox," just like adults do when they come home from work. Give them the space or at least expect them to take it (and don't take it personally when they do take the space—see Nick's comments in Chapter 2). At the same time, seize the moment if they do want to talk but don't expect it and *don't* hold it against them: "You told me all about your day yesterday, why not today?" As a general rule, if the conversation is forced and guilt-driven, it is probably detrimental to your relationship. If the conversation is freely offered, it can be quite valuable to your relationship. I recently got a call from a mom who took this idea to heart, so instead of resisting her daughter's desire for privacy she now encouraged it. "Hard day today? Why don't you get some juice and go listen to music in your room for awhile. It'll help you relax. I'll call you in about an hour for dinner, and we can catch up then." Since she discovered this new approach, things have quieted down significantly between her and her daughter, and the flow of information between the two has also improved.

Realize that it is not normal for sophomores to come home and want to brief their parents up on the details of their life. In many ways, high school is an elongated process of entering adulthood, which includes keeping certain aspects of one's life to oneself, and sharing those aspects when one chooses to do so.

> I was having big problems with my boyfriend and with my soccer coach, but instead of talking to my friends I talked to my mom. I know this sounds like a weird thing for a teen-ager to do, but it's just that only my mom would be willing to listen to everything I had to say and not feel obliged to give advice. She's cool that way.

Remember that many of your former methods of parenting aren't working anymore, and in fact, often make things worse. Most sophomores feel this dramatically, and desperately want more independence in their lives, all without losing you as an ally.

Consider this example. Stemming from the desire to assert their independence, every high school across the country has at least a couple of sophomores or juniors who experience what I call "The Party from Hell." The kid's parents are out of town for the weekend, and he invites a few friends over for a small party. Of course, the small party lasts for about ten minutes before two hundred of his closest friends hear about it and crash it, seemingly all at once. Eventually neighbors call in the police to halt the festivities, but usually not before several thousands of dollars in damage has been done: jewelry stolen, furniture destroyed, cars scratched, gardens ruined, and so on.

> It was pretty ugly for awhile. My parents were so pissed that they didn't speak to me for days. I've never seen my father and mother so mad. I felt like such a jerk. But to make a long story short it really worked out for us, after awhile. They grounded me indefinitely—from after school until the beginning of school the next day (it lasted for three months)—and every day one of them left work early to meet me after school and to stay with me. They took away my phone and obviously they took away use of the car. At first I went crazy. I didn't talk to them for a week. All the while I seriously thought about sneaking out at night and even made plans to run away. But I never did, and I'm not

really sure why, because I was really close a few times. I guess part of it was that after the first few days they didn't rub the party in my face anymore (except for a few times); they just stuck to the punishment. Eventually I got all my old privileges back, but it took a while. I'm real glad my parents didn't give up on me, like I've seen so many others do with my friends. And that was weird: none of my friends could understand why my parents were being so hard on me. They all thought it was way too extreme. It was hard for all of us, but it was worth it. But don't get me wrong, I wouldn't recommend it for other kids!

Fortunately, in this example both the parents and the teenager recognized that an underlying cause of the disaster was the difference in expectations of trust and honesty. The son hadn't trusted his parents enough to ask permission to have the party, and the parents had overindulged their son by giving him more freedom than he could handle. Afterward, their only recourse was to take the necessary time and energy to build that trust and honesty.

The preceding examples lay the groundwork for what a fair number of students experience as the "sophomore slump," which usually occurs in the latter part of tenth grade. Your adolescent is struggling to define herself and make her own choices. She wants to decide what is important to her and the kind of person she wants to be, yet at the same time she feels held back in making these decisions. She is both excited and cautious about taking control. A parent doesn't stand much of a chance under these circumstances. If you offer too much direction, she rebels; if you give her too much space, she rushes out past the limits. More than anything, she needs to feel that she is making meaningful decisions about the direction of her life. In many ways she is suffering from a brief existential crisis, something that most adolescents experience at some point during their high school careers. (See the letter at the conclusion of the next section on the junior year.)

I got in a lot of trouble for lying to my parents over the weekend. Actually, I got in trouble because I got caught lying. Anyway, I know that I blew whatever trust they had in me when I got caught. Now I have to earn back their trust. It's just that somehow I have to do it in a different way and as a different person. I have to be myself rather than just be out to please them. It's a little strange, but I know something has changed in me and I can't ignore it.

In the extreme, some sophomores consider transferring to another high school, in part for the new environment and in part to assert authority over their lives in a meaningful manner. Amazingly, even the largest of high schools is "small and boring" to most sophomores in the midst of this slump.

It came out of the blue. In March of her sophomore year, Lisa said she wanted to change schools. I was shocked. But rather than resist, I helped her think through the process of making such a decision, including visiting other schools and talking to teachers at her current school and potentially new schools. I also told her that I would prefer that she stay where she is, but if she really wanted to transfer and could make a good argument for her case then we would go along with her decision. In the end it was a close call, but she decided to stay.

Sophomores who consider transferring are essentially going through a reevaluation process that is vitally important, and one that all adolescents go through on some level. If the transfer question nags at them and they don't seriously explore it or are prohibited from exploring options, they'll often float through the remainder of high school without any solid conviction. If, however, they explore this question fully, in all its ambiguity and anxiety, chances are much greater that they'll be quite committed in their final two years of high school.

This reevaluation process can take numerous forms: changing friends, quitting or joining a sport, quitting or taking up a musical instrument, and so on. The solution to this crisis lies in teenagers making decisions and taking actions in areas that they feel are meaningful. They are beginning to chart their lives and need to start feeling responsible for their directions. In many ways, sophomore year comes in like a lamb and goes out like a lion. And for now, during her sopho-more year, your teenager will probably assert her independence by not telling you that she loves you—she has to reevaluate this assumption for herself.

Eleventh Grade

Junior year represents a significant change: the teenager is now official-ly an upper-class student. Physically, juniors have a much more accu-rate sense of and are more comfortable in their bodies. Cognitively, they are quite comfortable with abstract thinking. This is most evident at home, where they often challenge parents' ideas and rationales for certain behaviors.

> Up until last year I had no trouble holding my own [intel-lectually] with my daughter. But during this year [eleventh grade] things have changed, and I've got to scramble quite a bit to stay even with her. She asks some very tough ques-tions, that, along with some perceptive observations, are difficult to side-step. For instance, I stress honesty in rela-tionships. And the other day she overheard me fudging an answer to my boss on the phone. Later that night she con-fronted me on it. At first I tried to rationalize it away, but she quickly undid each rationalization until I was eventually quite frustrated and vulnerable. She finally just shook her head and walked away. It was an uncomfortable role reversal.

For students considering college, a new pressure is building steam: getting into college and the importance of grades during the junior year. College admission offices place great emphasis on the junior year and first semester of the senior year, as they believe they are the best indicators of a student's academic capabilities.

> Because junior year was great in most areas, the pressure about getting into college was a real drag. It was like it couldn't be avoided anymore, no matter how hard I tried.

In social matters, most juniors have achieved relative comfort, and are taking advantage of what is offered. With a driver's license and periodic access to a car, their social world has expanded. Now they are able to meet a crosstown buddy for a movie at a moment's notice. This access to a car is at times perplexing for parents who find their teenager with no specific destination on a weekend night.

> I'm not sure where we're going. Sean is going to pick us all up and we'll decide from there. We don't even know what is going on yet, so how can we know where we'll end up?! We'll just figure it out as we go. It's no big deal! You know, I'm not a little kid anymore.

This year is also the time for both more intimate and more diverse friendships. On the one hand, many teenagers are looking for closer and more satisfying friendships, building on those they had in sophomore year. They want to get beyond superficial acceptance with one another, but they're not sure how and with whom it is safe. Most are quite ripe for a significant romantic figure in their lives. On the other hand, they often want to spend time with diverse people: those who are different from them, and who were unavailable during freshman year because of restrictive friendship groupings. Teenagers are becoming more curious about people and their beliefs—though probably not with members of their own family. You may hear about a "brilliant statement" made by your daughter's English teacher or best friend's parent, only to somewhat gallingly realize that you told her the same thing several months ago and were met with utter disdain!

> Tracy is my youngest of four, so I'm long over the ego blow that goes with being the parent of a teenager. I know she is deaf to my most insightful offerings. But I also know that she adores her History teacher and hangs on every word he says. So I call him every few months and plant a few insights for him to offer should the time arise. I don't really care where she hears most of this stuff, as long as she hears it somewhere.

In their personal worldviews, juniors tend to be idealistic and somewhat romantic in the face of reality. This is both wonderful and painful to watch. They now must learn some of the hard lessons of human nature while you stand by, unable to help. These necessary life experiences come in a variety of places: first loves, best friends, academics, sports, dramatic or musical performances, and writing, to name a few. Adolescents are developing stronger personal identities while remaining quite fragile. All the while, they are discovering and exploring appropriate, and sometimes inappropriate, vehicles for their passions.

Finally, because they spend more and more time away from home, juniors are getting a clearer picture of the players in their family. Many begin to see their parents first as human beings and second as parents. They recognize and identify shortcomings and strengths in their immediate family. This can be a harsh reality until they learn compassion and acceptance, which usually doesn't happen until late senior year or, most likely, several years after high school is over.

> I remember naively noting at the end of my freshman year
> in college how much more intelligent and civil my father
> had become since my junior year in high school.

As mentioned in the "Tenth Grade" section, many teenagers undergo some sort of brief existential crisis in the latter stages of high school. Over the years, a number of students I've known have addressed this in what have been called "Letters of Independence" to their parents. In these letters, they congratulate their parents on raising them well, and inform them that their duties now must shift. They are declaring their independence, and they are doing so in a thoughtful and mature manner. In short, these letters start a whole new dialogue between parent and adolescent, and, most of all, allow all to participate gracefully. What follows is the type of letter I might write to students before they write their own Letter of Independence:

Dear _____:

This letter is an attempt to summarize the issues we discussed in our most recent conversation.

It seems that you and your parents are engaged in a struggle over your life—more specifically, who is in charge of your life. Your parents, in their efforts to help you succeed and be happy, are, according to your perspective, over-managing and over-directing your life. They are not trusting you with the decisions that you need to make, the decisions with which you feel you must be familiar and experienced in order to direct your life in a satisfactory manner.

Because they are over-managing, you are left in the defensive position of simply trying to get by. (You've also taken to a bit of under-managing in order to get their goat.) Unfortunately, this position doesn't encourage or allow you to start making your own priorities and decisions about what is important to you. By now you know very well what is important to your parents and the other adults in your world. These are the "should's" that fill your head and increase your feelings of guilt. Let's look at a few specifics.

Homework: Your parents constantly stress the importance of homework and good grades. They periodically "pop" into your room to check on how things are going, which often infuriates you. They also direct you when to do homework (of course, in your best interests, so that you can manage it all), while simultaneously criticizing your lack of time-management skills. Somehow they expect you to learn time-management skills without making any errors in the process. All in all, their attitude is one of mistrust in your ability and willingness to study on your own. For you this is particularly infuriating, as you care a great deal about your schoolwork and doing well. But with all their over-managing, your own cares and concerns have gotten pushed to the side. You hardly ever think about what you want—you usually spend your time thinking more about what you don't want.

Social Life: Your parents want you to have friends, but they don't want friends to interfere with your academic life. They will routinely say no to weekend nights out so that you have time to get your homework done. Unfortunately, they operate from a purely rational framework. For example, if you have plans for Saturday night then they insist you do your homework on Friday night, even though few if any students are capable of doing quality homework on a Friday night, given the accumulated stress and exhaustion caused by the week.

Time: In an effort to protect you from your poor time-management skills, your parents pay too much attention to how you spend your time. They routinely order an end to phone calls, direct you to your room after dinner to study, and inquire persistently about your homework progress. In short, they are limiting your ability to learn time management through the consequences of your own actions—good or bad.

Your Body: Again, with the best of intentions, they try to help out by reminding you not to eat too much, commenting on your style of dress, and offering unsolicited advice about appearance; none of this feedback gives you any sense of freedom of choice. Instead, you are often left in a reactionary and defensive position. Also, their indirect criticisms hurt you quite a bit.

Your Voice: By talking over you, your parents are in effect diminishing your ability to make and voice your own opinions about yourself, the future, and the world in general. Worse yet, this does not allow you to decide for yourself, in your own voice, what is truly important to you. In the long run, if your priorities aren't in your own voice, the necessary commitment and motivation you need to meet your goals are missing. This leaves you more worried about your parent's reactions to your life than about your own reactions to your life.

So, as we discussed, all this has left you feeling depressed because you are living your life for others, with a genuine lack of joy and self-direction in your life, always feeling like your "fuel tank" is near empty.

Still, it is clear that your parents love you and want what is best for you. The question is, can they get out of your way long enough and gracefully enough for you to discover and achieve what is best for you? Fortunately, this is where you have more influence than you might realize.

The point of this type of letter is not to decide who is right or wrong; rather, it is to encourage teenagers to take a lead in their lives and include their parents in a genuinely supportive role, which is good for everyone. If juniors and seniors don't have meaningful authority in their lives, they frequently turn to irresponsible authority, often risk-taking, with drugs, alcohol, and unsafe driving.

During junior year, your teenager may again be saying that he loves you, but adding that he also can't or won't tell you everything.

Twelfth Grade

Senior year is what most students have been waiting for. Now it is their turn to be the leaders of the school. High school has become their home, and they are quite comfortable there, though perhaps a bit restless too. In fact, much of senior year is spent alternating between and attempting to resolve these feelings of comfort and restlessness.

Because senior year is their last year, many feel the need to somehow make the high school experience meaningful so they don't walk away from these years "empty-handed." Meaning, if it has not come already, can come in a number of areas: sports, drama, academics, college admission, school newspaper, yearbook, prom committee, relationships, employment, student government, community service, or clubs. The important point is that by the conclusion of senior year, teenagers need to have found a place where they could leave a mark. With these goals motivating them, many enter senior year inspired to make this a different kind of year, and a better one than the previous three—which is quite a bit of pressure to put on oneself.

Senior year for me was a huge turning point. I became more outgoing and confident, and I really discovered who I am as a person. Remember, senior parents, we aren't abandoning you—in fact, we'll really miss you next year!

In this year, friendships take on even greater importance than in previous years, as the social scene is well known and well practiced. In fact, by the end of the year it is an old scene for most. Also, some have significant sexual and romantic relationships prior to or during this year, while others are pained to have not had such relationships. (See Chapter 9.)

At home, a great deal of ground has already been covered in the first three years. Teenagers have achieved a certain amount of autonomy, and how that was achieved is quite important. If it was a more-or-less graceful process, then parent and teenager are getting along fairly well and slowly preparing themselves for the inevitable separation that comes with graduation.

> Her sophomore and junior years were pretty rough. But to everyone's credit we all hung in there, so that by senior year we were actually on good terms with each other. It was kind of ironic; here we were saying hello to each other for really the first time—just as we were getting ready to say good-bye.

On the other hand, if the teenager hasn't secured a reasonable amount of autonomy or if the parents have given up on the adolescent, the senior year is a continuation and escalation of the previous years' problems.

> By senior year we were all at each other's throats. We had argued a great deal during the first three years but hadn't solved anything, so what else could we expect during senior year? We were stuck in a rut that wouldn't be broken until sometime after high school.

For college-bound students, the first semester of senior year means a lot of stress—in terms of schoolwork, college applications, and personal and family pressure. Non-college-bound students are also feeling stress but from slightly different sources—post-graduation decisions about employment, living situations, and, of course, personal and family pressure. They are also feeling the stress of being excluded when they listen to classmates plan for college (in spite of the fact that not going to college may be their own choice). They also experience their stress at a different rate than college-bound students. College-bound students feel the bulk of their future-related stress in the first semester; non-college-bound students experience the bulk of their future-related stress in the second semester.

For those aspiring to college, the academic pressure of the junior year continues to intensify throughout the first semester of the senior year. Suddenly everyone is interested in their future: parents are asking about school choices, inquiring about application deadlines and essays, stressing the importance of this semester's grades. The adults around them (teachers, relatives, and friends' parents) want to hear the list of schools to which they're applying. Remember how vulnerable adolescents are during this time. They are completing applications and putting themselves on paper for public judgment. It is quite a task.

> I know it's hard to deal with (and to deal with me), but I felt such a sense of denial throughout this whole college process that it made it very difficult for me to face all the things I had to do—deadlines, choices, etc. This not only frustrated my parents but also myself. But they need to know or recognize this sense of apprehension and denial.[1]

I once spoke to a parent who, anticipating the stress and drama around the college admissions process, decided to join in wholeheartedly. He chose to go through the same process as his son! He got information from various schools, made a list of his favorites, narrowed the list down according to the probability of admission (using his own high school grades and SAT scores), and completed the application process for all of them. He figured that school was a full-time job for his son, so that doing the application process in addition to his regular job was comparable to what his son was going through.

> The process is huge, much worse than when I applied to college. Just to be sure of getting into a school that I would be willing to attend, along with a few longshots, meant

applying to seven schools. My son and I were both burning the midnight oil the night before they were due! At first he was skeptical of what I was doing, and we hardly ever spoke of it. But when he saw that I was serious and not insulting in what I was doing, he began to get curious. From then on we spent time commiserating on how difficult the essays were; we even critiqued each other's essays along the way. All in all it didn't give me any more control or direct influence over the process, but it did provide two unexpected benefits. First, I developed a real compassion for what he was going through, which indirectly brought us closer in a manner I hadn't imagined. Second, I felt active in the process, which allowed me not to intrude so readily on his business.

I heartily recommend this exercise for interested parents.

For students who are not college-bound, the process is similar, though a bit less formal. Instead of colleges, they are thinking of jobs and living situations. And there is no set application or deadline for this process.

It's all kind of hard to think about because it seems so unreal. School just sort of ended, and then there was nothing to do. My parents were all over me to get a job, but I had no idea what I wanted to do. So for the most part I got together with my friends at night and partied, though there was this weird tension between those going to college and those of us who were staying home.

Students beginning their careers after graduation must figure out, in concrete terms, where and how they are going to get themselves started. Also, for most, home is getting small very quickly, so at the very least they have to somehow change their relationship to home as they get closer to moving out on their own.

Once I got a full-time job things began to change with my parents. It was rough for awhile. They wanted me to live by their rules in their house and I wanted them to leave me alone and treat me like an adult—I was paying them room and board and figured I was entitled to my freedom and privacy.

College-bound or not, getting "senioritis" during the second semester of senior year is a common experience for most high school students. To get through the intensity of first semester, most seniors dangle the carrot of second semester in front of themselves. They imagine this as a time of ultimate relaxation and enjoyment: the academic pressure is off; friends have time for one another; and they're the leaders of the school and running all the major functions. However, the reality is often a harsh one. Why is this so and how is senioritis experienced by many students?

Since second-semester grades are perceived as virtually ignored by colleges unless they are absolutely abysmal, students who have perceived high school primarily as a means of getting into college generally no longer care about grades. Unfortunately, the majority of students think this way. In effect, they feel they have earned the right to kick back, academically—and no amount of yelling, cajoling, or bribery is going to change that mind-set. Parents and teachers have minimal influence over this phenomenon once it has set in, primarily because the antidote must be applied before second semester is underway. If education is seen as an end unto itself, then less of a focus on grades and more on curiosity and self-directed learning is often fruitful. This is why projects and independent studies of the students' own choosing are often quite successful during the second semester of senior year. If, on the other hand, education is viewed as the means (grades) to the end (college), then once their college decision is secured they are, in effect, on vacation.

An articulate description of this kind of senioritis is described by one of William Mayher's students:

> Senior slump begins with the receiving of the first acceptance letter from college. I've been slumping since about February. School is no longer an academic hardship; it is a social gathering. It's a place where friends meet and go out to lunch and plan parties. School becomes a place to thrive

on your freedom. We are finally released from the bondage of a rigorous, forced secondary education. One loses the ability to concentrate, think, or comprehend what is taught. It's a time to daydream, doodle, fall asleep, or not even show up.

Not too many teachers remain empathetic with someone displaying this attitude in their classroom. Thus, rather than being regaled and extolled for their achievements (as many do fantasize), seniors are often chastised and reproached by both faculty and parents. Hardly what they expected: the most respected adults in their lives are annoyed and upset with them. In this vein, I know of several seniors who have expressed concern that their teachers take their behavior personally, when it is seldom intended that way, no matter how outrageous it appears.

> [When I skip class] I wish teachers would just mark me absent for the class and give me a zero for the day. I understand the consequences, but I don't need to be lectured as if it is a personal attack on them or something. I don't need that guilt along with everything else I'm feeling.

Second semester is not just another semester; it is a qualitatively different experience for the student. The end is not only within sight, it is unavoidable. This means simultaneously reengaging with friends and disengaging from the school and friends; it means preparing to leave a familiar environment to establish themselves all over again in a new environment; it means trying to have all the fun necessary to indeed make these "the best years of their lives"; and it means feeling compelled to understand themselves better than they already do. Again, one of Mayher's students said it well:

> It's difficult to pinpoint, but it's a weird period of ups and downs. One moment it can be diagnosed as spring fever; you feel elated, feel the desire to "get out." The next moment you are down, lethargic, lacking energy. The paper you have to hand in to graduate seems to be an impossibility.

Whether up or down you feel an overall lack of ability to concentrate. Your mind wanders; you think of the prom, of graduation, of leaving your friends. How can you realistically concentrate on the "core collapse theory" with those ideas racing around in your head?

I think that senior slump is just a normal part of adolescence. It's part of the transition period from the teenage years to adulthood and it's one of the few ways that kids know how to deal with separation. After attending this school for as many years as most of us have, it no longer matters whether you have enjoyed your experience here or not. Graduation is painful. You are leaving the familiar to go out into the unknown (corny as that sounds). What I think that most people don't realize is that senior slump is a deeper concept than people realize. It goes beyond ceasing to care about grades you get on tests and what you're learning in school. And it's not that you no longer care about these things because you are into college and learning isn't important.

You don't stop learning when you hit senior slump; rather, you use the fact that the pressure is off you to learn more about yourself. I know I feel the need now more than ever "to find myself" before I go to college. It's like a giant mishmash; you have to untangle yourself from your high school years, find the pieces of you that are mixed up with everyone else, collect yourself, and go to college. At the same time you know that you have left something of yourself there in the mishmash because you can't find every piece, but you learn to accept this. That's what senior slump is all about. It's not a disease; it's a healthy, normal reaction to what's happening all around you.

So, as a parent, what are you apt to see at home? First of all, your teenager will push for greater independence in the form of more lenient curfews, going out on school nights, going on weekend trips with friends, and doing less and less homework—all with more moodiness than usual.

> As the end of senior year nears , all you want is out—it doesn't mean the experience in high school was horrible; it just means you're ready for a change. Once you've worked hard for three and a half years, you want a break—and rightfully deserve one. That doesn't mean being a flake; it just means going out when the time seems good (yes, on school nights).

Second, your teenager may develop a greater focus on friends and crises in their lives. Emotional catastrophes may appear that demand their immediate attention and that they will be extremely hesitant to explain. It is quite common for family and personal difficulties that have remained in the background throughout high school to suddenly command center stage as the senior year winds down, and typically it is friends that one turns to first and foremost. Every year, in the six weeks that precede graduation, a number of seniors visit me to "unpack" some of this stuff in order to repack it more efficiently and with less emotional weight. (See Chapter 2 and the section on Family for more on this topic.)

By the end of this year, your teenager is once again telling you that she loves you.

Endnote

1. This quote, along with several others in this chapter, is excerpted from William S. Mayher, "The Dynamics of Senior Year: A Report From the Frontlines."

Table 1: Summary of the High School Years

	Ninth	Tenth
Physical and Cognitive	Girls are ahead of the boys; How do I fit in?; do I dress/talk/act right?; lots of emerging sexual energy; shifting into abstract thinking; need to develop study skills; new relationship with teachers.	Boys beginning to catch up; anything within normal is tolerable, otherwise is dismal; some girls flirting with eating disorders and boys "bulking up"; lots of sexual energy; still unsure of how to relate to adults; are academics important to me?
Social	Lots of new and unfamiliar classmates; must find a niche; where and with whom to eat lunch?; party scene, yes or no?	I have people to hang with, but are they real friends?; do I want to transfer?; party scene, yes or no?; natural groups via interests: sports, drama, school government, etc.
Friendship	Want people to spend time with; groupings by similarities; initial anxiety to have friends; cling to old or make new friends?	Do my friends want the same kind of friendship as I do?; are we changing in similar or different manners; life would be terrific if only I had a boy/girlfriend!; need good friends as I grow away from family.
Personal Identity	Am I myself?; seeming lack of structure to find myself in (compared to middle school); loneliness and grief over lost identity of middle school; developing self-consciousness; emerging sexuality.	Do I like who I am; whose fault is it?; I want and should be in charge of myself, shouldn't I?; What is important to me?; who am I, besides not my parents?; sexuality and extreme self-consciousness.
Family Events	Begin to feel the need to renegotiate relationship with parents; old events are re-considered, *i.e.* divorce and issues of custody; talk to friends about family events.	Can't wait to drive; serious re-negotiating of parent roles; they are fired as managers and working hard to become my consultant on my terms; I can talk about family issues with my friends.

Table 1 (continued)

Eleventh	Twelfth
Boys are caught up; everyone becoming more relaxed, in fact working very hard to be relaxed; eating and body image issues; Future pressures in present; what is after high school?; college and work questions: external and internal pressure around the importance of this year; whose decision is this anyway?; lots of sexual energy.	Beginning to feel comfortable; the oldest and biggest in the school; lots of sexual energy; work like hell and then life's a beach; reality of college and future; I will be judged; leaving secure and known academic environment—both good and bad.
I'm here, for better or worse; getting bored with social scene, strong desire for closer friends; more serious experimentation.	Leaving secure social environment—both good and bad; somewhat bored with present and anxious about the future.
Close friends often changing or deepening; life would be terrific if only I had a boy/girlfriend!; changing relationships to adults and authority figures.	Very close to friends and have to leave them; what will our friendship be in the future? Can I ever make new friends as close as these high school friends?
Idealistic and often romantic in face of reality; stronger sense of self, but it is so fragile and ever-changing; lots of shoulds and guilt at unmet expectations; strong sexuality.	Reflecting and learning, and reacting and behaving; I'm just getting a handle on myself; I'm either ready to go or scared to go—probably both.
I'm driving and experimenting more; want to be seen as more adult and responsible; can seriously question parents and their choices.	I'm leaving home; preparing the way for the new relationship with parents—the post-high school relationship; re-examining past issues of family prior to next phase of life.

❧ CHAPTER 4 ❧

Graduation

What can I expect from graduation?

The close of the high school years is a complex time, whether the student chooses to pursue college or not. Issues of dependence and independence intertwine as the new graduates get ready to go off on their own. They have reached a significant life marker; for many the formal entrance into the adult world or, at the very least, a more adult-like world. Also, with graduation comes a variety of inevitable experiences and confusion regarding identity and readiness which parents are unable to (and should not try to) resolve for their kids.

On the one hand, most high school students are pleased to have completed high school; are more or less satisfied with their performance; and are looking forward to beginning a more independent life. Many are thankful that high school is finally over, as they feel more than ready to move on with their lives. On the other hand, they are reluctant to leave a place that they know well, where they have a known and accepted identity, where they have created many happy and sad memories, and where they grew a great deal. And to complicate this, many are secretly wondering if they are indeed ready to be out there in the "real world," but since they've been talking it up for so long and because they can't leave too much room for self-doubt, they are reluctant to voice any misgivings, especially to parents.

> I've been ready for graduation since the beginning of senior year. I mean, by then I had basically done all that I wanted to do in high school. I don't mean to sound arrogant but it's true. I'm really ready to be on my own. But at the same

time there is this nagging doubt in the back of my head.
Sometimes I lie awake at night in fear of going away, making new friends, and doing it all over again. What if I'm not
as good as I think I am? And there is no way I can tell my
parents about it—they would freak out!

For parents, this is a similarly complex and confusing time. They
are proud of their teenager's successful completion of high school and
they are excited at the prospect of their adolescent becoming an adult,
but they are also apprehensive that maybe their child is not quite ready
for the "adult world." They are not sure how they are personally going
to handle their adolescent moving away from home, if that's the next
step. Parents often feel a compulsion toward perfection before their
child leaves home—what amounts to a kind of last-minute cramming
of all the "right lessons." Resist this tendency; it never works.

Some parents also feel the need to regress to behavior they used
when they had more control of the situation. For instance, curfew may
suddenly sweep back several hours to what it was when their teenager
was a freshman, with the only justification being: "Because I said so!
And as long as you live in my house you'll follow the rules of this
house!" Or, as one student said of his parents, "It's as if they're trying
to fit in all their parenting in these last few weeks when what I need is
room and time to absorb and deal with all that's been happening." And
as one parent said of his son, "I'm ready for him to go to college; I'm
just not ready for him to leave high school."

With all of this (and the points raised in the "Family" section of
Chapter 2), it's no wonder that many households undergo a fair share
of stress and arguing around graduation time. This arguing is often a
result of the excitement and anxiety that comes with change; it can also
be a means of parents and child moving away from one another in
preparation for the next phase.

During the second semester of my senior year I was a real
jerk to my teachers at school and to my parents at home. I
was moody and angry most of the time. I argued with
teachers about assignments, skipped school, went to school
stoned, and played rude pranks on people. At home I was

even worse. I don't know why. I was just angry at everyone around me. Everyone was relieved by the time I graduated. But a couple of years later I came back to school for a basketball game. It was the first time I had been back since graduation. And I know it sounds corny, but all of a sudden it made sense: I had felt like I was being thrown out of high school (where I had done well before second semester of senior year). So, rather than get tossed out, I unconsciously decided to reject *them* first. I really loved high school, but I had been too scared about leaving to face up to it. Somehow it was easier to get angry.

This young man's reaction gives an idea of all the changes teenagers are trying to integrate during and immediately after graduation. This is not to say, however, that they are separating from home. Separation implies a breaking away and disconnection; a better description is that they are extending themselves away from family and friends. This extension allows them the room to grow *and* maintains the vital family connection. More than anything, graduation requires a thorough updating of close relationships.

When my parents and sister dropped me off at school, they stayed a few hours and helped me set up my room. It was nice, but still I was itching for them to leave. Anyway, when they did leave I walked them to the parking lot and gave everyone hugs—we all sniffled a bit too, which kind of surprised me. My dad was last, but before I could turn away to leave he handed me a cassette and said, "We all love you." When I played the cassette it was a message from my parents and my sister. Basically they each said what they were going to miss about me, what they weren't going to miss about me, and how they thought college would affect me. It was mind-blowing! I must have listened to that tape twenty times during that first semester. In fact, I still have it. Oh yeah, my dad also managed to tuck a few $20s into the cassette case, which was cool.

When your adolescent goes away to college (or moves far away from home), I suggest giving her a disposable camera. Have her take lots of photos of her living space and the people around her, then ask her to send the whole camera home. (It is best to give her a SASE.) The photos will help you accurately imagine your adolescent in her new home. Anything like this that allows for full extension without disconnection is helpful.

What follows is a graduation message that all parents should hear. In a commencement speech at San Francisco's University High School in 1993, Joe DiPrisco speaks as a poet, a member of the faculty, and the parent of a graduating senior.

Commencement 12 June 1993

...It's time to get down to business. Or, to quote Groucho Marx when, as the lunatic explorer Captain Spaulding in *Animal Crackers*, he sang, "Hello, I must be going."

Which, as they say while being interrogated in the old detective movies, is my story, and I'm sticking to it.

You know, psychologists, who seem to have names for everything, label this sort of thing (the Hello-I-must-be-going sort of thing, the Come-here-go-away sort of thing) a double message.

Of course, there are double messages and double messages; poets depend for their existence upon double messages, saying one thing and meaning another, but so do politicians and bureaucrats, saying one thing and doing another. Still, we human beings must have either a magnificent tolerance or a tremendous need for such doubleness. If you think about it, any good class is predicated upon doubleness—discussing one thing, while treating another. We are reading or performing Shakespeare, or studying Vietnam, or the Bible, or American Literature, but we are simultaneously reading, and maybe even performing, ourselves, simultaneously examining the grounds of our own understanding of ourselves, our community, our world. Of course, the whole bittersweet secret to high school is that we're not simply COVERING material—books, texts, ideas, themes, whatever; at the same time we are also discovering, uncovering ourselves, our values, the sources of our senses of meaning.

Even so, this is our common task today, at commencement, to say in some fashion to each other, "Hello, we must be going." In a matter of minutes we are out of here, some of us for the summer, some of us for what seems like forever, but in the very moment of disengaging, perhaps we might find ourselves more engaged than ever before. Perhaps, moving away from each other, we might find ourselves growing a bit closer. There goes that doubleness again.

But before you graduate, a word or, I guess I should say, two. Isn't it strange that, though your guardians and parents and teachers have had you in their care, so to speak, for some time now, we will probably be unable to resist the temptation to give you just a few more pointers on the use and misuse of this education, this life, this world.

Since commencement speeches should have some high, redeeming social purpose, I hope to show you how to read the doubleness of these last-minute exhortations. As you go forth into that wondrous world beyond high school, you will hear profound thoughts volunteered by your family and friends, deep insights into the human condition, learned admonitions, savvy propositions gained at the expense of hard-won experience, such as:

1. Don't leave your clothes unattended in the laundromat. Amazing, how otherwise competent people with fascinating stories, inspiring vocations, and intelligently diversified investment portfolios and social consciences will exhibit an unquenchable interest in the state of your laundry. You may assume that "Don't leave your clothes unattended in the laundromat" means "Let's not spend any more at The Gap." But actually on another level, translated, this means, though we wish it weren't true, that sometimes the world is a nest of spiders; sometimes people are going to let you down. But if

perfect strangers will prove capable of mind-boggling, heart-breaking indifference, and cruelty, these same strangers may also exhibit shocking tenderness. Because translated, this means, when you do leave your clothes overnight in the dryer, as you will, who knows, you may return to discover that someone has folded everything crisply, and left you another, more beautiful shirt. Translated, this means, it's okay when you mess up. Be ready for the small miracles and the genuine good luck that may, for no good earned reason, come your way.

2. Don't change a flat tire on the highway. Translated, this means, don't drive your car or anybody's car too fast, too slow, too long without factory-authorized professional maintenance or without fuel; don't drive in front of, behind, or alongside a truck, a motorcycle, a bike, a bus, or any another moving or stationary vehicle; don't drive in the first light, or under the noon sun, or after darkness falls, or when it's raining, or snowing, or windy. In fact, if you can arrange it, we'd appreciate it if you didn't drive at all. And while we're on the subject, don't use any form of transportation, public or private. Translated, all this ultimately means is, slow down, what's the hurry, where are you going, take some long walks by yourself, settle the scores within yourself before you take them up with anybody else. Translated, this means, some risks are worth taking, and some are simply not. Translated, this means, travel far but travel well, remembering occasionally what Thoreau said, about traveling widely, all over a small place known as Walden Pond. Translated, this means, sometimes, in the middle of a fantastic accident, hitting the freeway divider at full speed, you wake up in mid-air, see your life pass before your eyes, float upside-down to the asphalt on the wings of what have to be angels, and walk away, without a scratch.

3. Please, please, please don't get a dog. Translation: Soon as you are ready, get a really good dog. I personally recommend a mixed-breed dog in the neighborhood of seventy to eighty

pounds, and I suggest naming this dog after a character in a nineteenth-century novel. This will serve as a trusty conversation starter, and will always remind you of your intellectual roots—though conceivably to your embarrassment. Translated, this means, at the same time, that we wish for you just a little bit of loneliness—not so much that you doubt your worth, and not so little that you never experience a test of your character. As a supercilious poet once remarked, the only cure for loneliness is solitude. Don't forget, a good dog is very good company in solitude. Translated, in addition, this means we hope that you will make good and strong friends, that you never take for granted the loyalty and love of your friends.

4. Don't play in a poker game organized by the slowest, but, gee, the nicest guy you think you know. This literally means, you are about to become the breakfast of champions. Translated, on another level, this means take up an interest others may find esoteric, quaint, or odd as soon as possible, like fly-fishing, billiards, Classical Greek; become an expert in James Joyce, or roses, or pottery, or Elizabethan poetry, or jazz, or most especially birds, which reward intense interest with supreme, gorgeous apathy, sometimes a necessary thing to endure. Translated, this also means, be suspicious of all received opinion, all the conventional views. Think your own thoughts as far as you are able, make your own mistakes, take your own chances.

5. Once you get settled in, drop us a line, or call up, anytime, day or night. Translation: This seemingly obvious one could refer to the subtlest mystery of all. It isn't about keeping tabs on you, it isn't about control. Translated, philosophically speaking, this means, we don't truly know how we're going to get along without you.

6. Don't study all night long. Translation: All-nighters are uplifting for the soul. Studying by the midnight oil (whatever that is), or frantically composing papers at the very last minute is very good for the soul, if not necessarily in the

short-term interests of the body. I mean, do you care, do you really care to put it all together? This may be something as of yet that you do not know about yourself, and it will be terrific to find out, that you care this much, this deeply. But commit yourself to discovering the truth of an idea, to braving the consequences of your desire to master and to explain; there are few things more exhilarating than the pursuit of knowledge. Translated, this means, too, when you stay up all night, take a good look at the sunrise, which has now been somehow earned by you, the bands of pink and grey across the horizon, and notice carefully the way the early air smells of new snow, or fresh rain, or the turning of a season. Despite everything, the world is a beautiful and amazing place, all the more beautiful and amazing for your noticing it, and for your being in it.

7. Don't meet Professor Peach for a late-night cappuccino. The precise translation of this is: Don't meet Professor Peach for a late-night cappuccino.

8. Get ready for Number Eight, because we always stuff everything in this Number Eight steamer trunk. Just take the warm coat. Play defense with your feet. Eat your greens. Don't argue with a fool. Never make the third out at third base. Don't put on your socks in a dark room. Pay no attention to the man behind the curtain—lions and tigers and bears, oh my. Opposition is true friendship. Learn how to cook perfect scrambled eggs. Death to comma splices. Don't make every assertion end with a rising intoNATION? and question MARK? Live beneath the open sky and dangerously. Sound a barbaric yawp. Hate flattery and flatterers with a pure and constant heart. Don't believe the hype. And, don't forget, take that coat. Translation: We hope we gave you a few clues, we hope we have given you a head start. A head start on what? That would be hard to say. No family is without flaws, and you can't leave any school without taking a few scars. Translated, this injunction has something to do with love, that unmanageable thing. For the world can be a

cold and broken place. Translated, this means, fix the prisons. Fix the schools. Fix the cities. Fix the government. Fix the sky, the sea, the earth. Translated, this means, write the strong novel, break the tough story, build the beautiful building, sing the pure song, paint the essential painting, heal the sick, feed the hungry, shelter the homeless, teach the children. Give blood, give your time, give yourself.

9. You sure you're ready for a big-time romantic relationship? Right. What an altogether useful, sensible piece of advice. As everybody knows, the typical adult has been the paragon of decorum, for the last seven-and-a-half minutes, anyway. But beyond that, translated, Number Nine means, better a too-serious, committed relationship than the other sorts, because—and we don't know how to take the edge off this, and here goes—because we are terrified of AIDS. And we are more terrified if we don't know that you are just a little bit terrified, too. Translated, this also means that we wish you good fortune, that you won't be hurt as much as you probably will be, and we wish that you are capable of being hurt, even if we don't wish that you do feel the knives of this disappointment. Strictly speaking, translated, we still find it impossible to understand how you could love anyone else— but we promise to try.

Finally, number 10. Be good. I don't know how to break this, but "be good" is technically untranslatable. Of course, be safe as you can be without letting life pass you by; of course, be kind as long as kindness does not enable you to compromise your principles. (And by the way, if you don't have any absolute principles—and absolute principles may seem pretty hard to come by in this monstrously relativistic postmodern moral universe we have created in the twentieth-century—try out a few, and practice, practice, practice.) Of course, be great if that's your fate, but if you are doomed to be great you probably can't avoid it anyway. But you know, being good could be tougher than being great; it certainly doesn't mean be recklessly careful, or polite, or conciliatory.

Don't be afraid of conflict; if there's no cause, no dream, no person worth fighting for, and fighting over, then who are you? As you can tell, if you get Number 10, you can forget Numbers 1 through 9, because Number 10 is what it's really all about. So be good.

There's more, but never mind.

You see, at this moment of moving away from each other, we may finally enjoy enough distance to see each other in plain relief. If this experience has not already occurred to you, it may happen today on the lawn of Julius Kahn Park, or at some celebration this afternoon, or across a restaurant table this summer, or at some noisy airport this fall, or in the crowded hallway of some dormitory during orientation— and we will see each other in an altogether new, suddenly much more available light. It promises to be an astonishing moment—even if we've been preparing for this surprise for the last seventeen, eighteen years.

Sometimes, in the middle of a class discussion, you make a point, you share an insight, you ask a question that breaks open everything, and I hear myself spontaneously uttering exactly what I am thinking, which is—I'm glad you came to school today. Even now, right now, I suggest you are giving witness to just that kind of insight, asking just such a perfect question, and so—and I mean this—no double message here—each and every one of you, thank you, thank you, thank you for coming to University High School today.

❧ CHAPTER 5 ❧

Limits and Structure

Are there any rules or guidelines that are guaranteed to work with teenagers?

Like just about everything else about teenagers, this question doesn't have a direct or simple answer. The question is really asking about limits and structure, which are very family-specific, and are thus difficult to discuss usefully in the abstract. Fortunately, many topics addressed in this book give concrete examples of what we'll be discussing in this section. But for now, what exactly is meant by "limits and structure," at least in terms of parenting? Basically, these terms refer to providing security for adolescents through consistency, clear expectations, appropriate guidelines, direct feedback, acknowledgement, and the separation of consequences and moral lessons. Only when teenagers experientially understand and trust the structure around them are they able to fully develop. The structure provides the safety in which they can suspend momentarily the inherent self-consciousness of adolescence; in other words, the structure contains the effects of anxiety on their development. This in turn opens the door for genuine curiosity, self-reflection, and learning.

Now, what does all this mean in practical terms? First, what it doesn't mean is that you use the same rules and limits with your tenth grader that you did when he was three years younger. His world has changed, so the rules and limits must reflect these changes. Throughout a person's growth, infancy through adulthood, structure and limits need to evolve to reflect each developmental stage. For instance, you wouldn't negotiate with a one-year-old about bedtime. Nor would you insist that your seventeen-year-old be in bed by 9:00 p.m. every night. These are not developmentally appropriate limits. Ideally, limits and structure form the foundation of the stable platform that adolescents use to launch themselves into adulthood. Realize that these rules include not only the actual guideline, but also the consistent enforcement and follow-through. Consistency between words and action is crucial, because no matter what you say about limits, it is what you do that truly matters.

> My parents are pretty clear with me about rules and expectations. But whenever they tell me something, I do the translating myself. Like if they say to be in by midnight, I know that if I'm in by 12:15 nothing is said; at 12:30 something is said and nothing is done; after 12:30 something is said and done.

Here, while words and actions don't quite match up, there is an underlying consistency that the adolescent understands. Without this, there is no way for the teenager to accurately "translate." In fact, consistency is so important that in some instances consistent "bad" parenting is better than extreme inconsistency between "bad" and "good" parenting.

> By most standards I guess my parents are pretty awful. They don't seem real interested in me other than the grades I get and the free baby-sitting I provide for my sisters. They hardly ever check up on me or ask about where I go at night. They always say to be in by 1:00 a.m., but they're never around to check, never mind enforce it. I don't think they want to be bothered. The only times they get upset are when I get in trouble at school and they get called, and of course when I leave dirty dishes on the counter. It isn't much compared to most of my friends, but at least I know what to expect. At least they're not constantly changing the rules on me depending on their mood at the time, like with some of my other friends. It is hard, but I'm learning to accept it. They're not going to change, that's for sure!

A good example of an enforced limit versus a literal limit is the 55-mile-per-hour speed limit on most freeways. While the actual speed limit is 55 miles per hour, many people have internalized an enforced speed limit of 60 to 61 miles per hour. Thus, if you get a ticket for going 64 miles per hour you'll be upset but you won't feel unjustly treated. But if you got a ticket going 57 miles per hour, you would feel unjustly treated.

It's best to make sure that the guidelines and rules you set for your adolescent are consistent with your own values. They ought be what you feel are appropriate and thus have little trouble enforcing. Too many parents set unreal expectations for themselves and their teenagers.

> At first we tried to be the perfect parents. We read all the how-to books and talked to lots of other parents about homework time, curfews, driving privileges, etc. Very quickly we had a clear set of rules that I'm sure the experts would have been proud of. But just as quickly that nice set of rules became undone, mainly because in our hearts we didn't really believe in them. Oh, we believed in them in theory, but in our day-to-day reality we wouldn't follow them. We had set our expectations too high. For example, at first we said no talking on the phone until all your homework is done. But in reality both my wife and I call our friends after dinner and before we do any leftover work from the office so that didn't seem fair. Also, it is more important to us for our daughter to learn how to be responsible for herself and her homework than to learn to follow our rules blindly. So we've edited our initial rules down to the ones that are important to us. Maybe we don't have the "best" rules in the world, but at least they're honest ones.

Unrealistic guidelines lead to inconsistent communication and enforcement, which means instability for the adolescent. Given the nature of the teenage world, instability is quite a severe handicap. (See Chapter 2.)

Establishing an appropriate structure is complicated by the fact that adolescence is a very different stage of development from others.

You can't simply upgrade the strategies and structures that worked from infancy through late childhood; they must be reworked for teenagers. In addition, there needs to be room for real input from adolescents. Through negotiation they learn to have more say and autonomy over their lives, a critical task in adolescence, and eventually to take on responsibility.

So, how does one decide on appropriate limits? The easiest way I know of is to work backward. Start by imagining the time teenagers leave home, either to go to college or to start their work life, when they are roughly eighteen years old. At this point they will be pretty much on their own, at least relative to their lives to date. What kind of decisions do they need to have experience making? What skills must they possess? How do they acquire these skills? What kinds of experiences (read *mistakes*) are necessary to learn all this? After you've reflected on this, move backwards to the present. Your reflections will guide you in developing appropriate structures and limits. (See Chapter 7 for more on this.)

> I learned the lesson between over-parenting and helping to prepare my oldest for the adult world in a rather shocking manner. I definitely over-parented. When he went off to college he couldn't do laundry, had never balanced a checkbook or made a budget, and didn't know how to clean a bathroom! Never mind the more personal skills of budgeting time, setting priorities, and making compromises such as negotiating with roommates. Believe me, his younger brother is getting plenty of opportunities for experience in these areas before he gets out of this house!

Without the gradual exposure to these types of experiences, adolescents must face them all at once, which is often overwhelming.

> I'm in charge of the freshmen dormitories at "X" University. Believe me, it's easy to see who was overprotected by parents. They're typically the ones that get lost in confusion or go self-destruct with all the freedom. They party, stay up late, skip classes, and generally dig themselves into a deep hole in the first semester. The freedom is too much for them; they seem to drown in all the choices.

During our Resident Advisor training we even do a session on how to spot these students and intervene in a useful manner. Most get it together by second semester. The ones that don't usually take a semester off, or sometimes leave for good.

The ideas of limits and structure are at least as important during adolescence as they are during any other previous growing-up period. By nature, human beings are curious limit-testers. It is our nature to explore the outer edges of our existence. Teenagers are no different. Before they can relax and settle into something, they need to understand and experience the exact parameters of the environment. Their testing is a means of exploring the limits. Expect the testing; in fact, be wary when it isn't there! And as difficult as it may be, don't take it personally.

> Every year it's exactly the same. At the beginning of the year I pass out a syllabus along with my rules for the class. We go over each one of them during our first meeting. The one that really gets them is: "Be on time or not at all." Basically, I close the door with the bell at the beginning of the class; if they are late without a written excuse they don't get in and they get a zero for the day. A simple, no-nonsense rule. Everyone understands it and is on time, at least for the first few weeks. Then I get the Test. Often the person least-likely to be late is the Tester. Typically they show up thirty seconds late without the required written excuse, but with a bag full of "legitimate reasons." Needless to say, after I send them away, to the shock of their classmates, there is hardly another incident for the duration of the semester. And if there is, the consequence is taken with minimal grumbling.

As adults we do the same kinds of testing—though usually, but not always, in more subtle ways.

The difficulty in holding consistent and appropriate limits with adolescents is that, developmentally, they are better-equipped than ever to test, sneak around, and argue with you and your logic. Thus, parents tend to head in one of two directions. The first is to become over-rigid, with the structure becoming symbolic of the battle of wills between you and your teenager. In this extreme, the trash must be taken out when you say so, without the least amount of hesitation. The second tendency is over-flexibility, with the structure as an implied reality, but with no real limits. In this extreme, you never mention the trash to your teenager; rather you take it out yourself because you can't ever imagine it happening any other way, and besides, it isn't worth arguing over. Both are equally disastrous to the adolescent's development. That is, as alluded to earlier, the manner in which they negotiate and compromise around these limits and rules is quite reflective of their level of maturity and responsibility. When kids are able to negotiate and take stands responsibly, the whole parent-adolescent relationship shifts. Parents need to be on the lookout for these changes.

> You won't believe what happened the other night with me and my parents! It was totally cool. As you know, I've been sick and tired of them treating me like a twelve-year-old all the time: telling me when to do my homework, telling me to pick up my room, telling me to get off the phone, telling me what to eat and what not to eat, etc. Well, finally I couldn't take it any more. So last night I told them that I was sixteen years old and if they wanted me to act sixteen then they needed to stop treating me like a twelve-year-old and start treating me like a sixteen-year-old. I didn't give them any examples; instead I said that I was sick of them running my life, and that I wanted my life back in my own hands. I was really pissed so I figured all hell would break loose after I finished, but to my shock they both smiled and said that it was about time! They had been waiting for me to say something for the past six months! I couldn't believe it! It's funny, that happened last week and things have been much better between them and me, and it's not that they are doing things all that different. It is just that they see me differently and as a result I understand them better. Pretty weird, huh?

Again, the negotiated limits and structure are your greatest sources of accurate feedback about your teenager's current level of maturity.

One final point on the difficulty of limits and structure. Because your kid is an adolescent, you have much less direct control over her, and she knows it. If she decides to go against your guidelines and to skip class, go to an unchaperoned party, stay out past curfew, and so on, there is not much you can do—short of physical intervention (not usually recommended) or calling the police. But over the long run don't discount the importance and influence of your opinions and ideas. They matter a great deal, which is why they are so important to articulate—though they are equally important not to belabor.

> My parents tell me exactly where they stand on all sorts of issues, but they leave me free to make my own decisions, though not necessarily with their approval. They're even willing to discuss things with me—real discussion. It wasn't always this way, though. During ninth and tenth grades I didn't tell them anything. I lied all over the place and they never caught on. But after a while it got to where we couldn't talk anymore—at least about anything beyond the local news or weather. I had told so many lies that I was scared that I might tip them off. You know, like asking them about a movie that they saw that I was supposed to have seen. Anyway, I got tired of it all one night. I was miserable with my friends and had nowhere to turn. So I sat them down and told them that I lied most of the time. I even told them some of the lies, but they didn't want to hear too many. We stayed up most of that night talking and things, but in the end it was like this giant brick wall had been taken down. It's much easier this way.

CHAPTER 6

Natural Consequences

*What are fair punishments when
teenagers break the rules? For instance,
how effective is "grounding"?*

The principle of natural consequences comes into play here. As a consultant-parent you have established a punishment that is a natural consequence of the offense.[1] For example, if the transgression involves a misuse of, deceitful use of, or irresponsible use of the car, then the natural consequence focuses on some type of restriction involving the car. In an ideal world, this natural-consequences principle of handling periodic slip-ups is spelled out with your child in a variety of settings and throughout his pre-adolescent years, so that he has somewhat internalized the principle by the time the car is a discussion point (of course, don't expect him to thank you for helping him to learn responsibility and the consequences of his actions when he comes in late on Friday night and loses the privilege of using the car before a big Saturday date).

By focusing on the natural consequences of an act—or as natural as possible—you become the enforcer of consequences in a consistent world, rather than the all-powerful (and resented) judge and jury in an unpredictable world. How would you like it if you appeared in traffic court to argue your $150 speeding ticket and found the arresting officer acting as judge and jury, not only deciding against your innocence but also tripling the fine! This is exactly how it feels to teenagers when consequences are chosen arbitrarily or when they aren't privy to the logic of the consequences.

The focus on natural consequences allows you to at least reduce and often sidestep many of the power issues of the adult-adolescent relationship, which are often the source of extended rifts between adults and adolescents. As a colleague of mine, Ray Greenleaf, is fond of saying, "The fight is hardly ever about who takes out the trash. The underlying struggle is more typically about power, more specifically, about who is in charge."* The beauty of natural consequences is that they skirt the power issue; the adolescent is in charge, because the consequences are a natural outcome of their actions or non-actions. You simply support the law of cause and effect.

A month or so after an evening meeting with a group of parents of eleventh graders, a mother called with this story of natural consequences and her son.

> It was Halloween night, a Friday to boot. Mark (sixteen years old), was going out with some of his buddies. He said they didn't have any particular plans; there were a few parties and things to check out, but anyway he would be home by 1:00. Nothing was unusual except that I realized, after he had left, that he was dressed in really beat-up clothes and they were all riding in one kid's pickup, something I hadn't known them to do before. I didn't know what to make of it, so I filed it away to ask Mark when he got home. Well, as things turned out, I didn't have to ask.

> Around midnight I got a call from the local police. They had Mark and a couple of his buddies down at the station for throwing eggs at cars from the back of the pickup! It seems they hit a pretty fast sports car that managed to get their license plate number. No charges were being formally made; the owner simply wanted to teach the kids a lesson and to get reimbursed for the necessary wash-and-wax job. I was stunned, and for some reason I apologized to the

---

* A useful question to ask yourself after a seemingly ridiculous argument with your adolescent is: "What in our relationship is this fight really about?" It may take a while and a few different circumstances to answer, but when you do get an answer it is well worth the effort.

officer. I also told him I would be there in ten minutes to get Mark. But something didn't feel right, so I called the officer back with a few questions of my own. Basically I learned that Mark didn't yet know that the officer had gotten in touch with me, and furthermore that the station was pretty busy that night with a usual weekend assortment of crimes and criminals. To make a long story short, I told the officer to tell Mark that he couldn't reach me and that he would try again later. I also told him that I would come and get Mark in a couple of hours, after he had a few hours to himself in the station without his friends. The officer chuckled and said he would "entertain" Mark until then.

To say the least, when I got Mark he was real pleased to see me. Basically I didn't have to say much, and not-so-surprisingly he was more than willing to suffer just about any consequence I had in mind!

Let's examine this more closely. If the mom had picked up her son right away, what might have been lost? First, she wouldn't have had time to reflect on what had actually happened. That is, without time the natural parental response is to overreact to your son being picked up by the police, but with time she came to see the incident for what it was—her son was facing the societal consequences of his actions, and thankfully, nobody had been hurt. Second, with this time she was able to separate herself personally from Mark's actions. Remember how she apologized to the officer when he called? Third, because she took this time (after assuring herself of his health and safety) it allowed Mark to uncomfortably sit with his consequences. And really, this is the only way he is going to learn the idea of natural consequences, and subsequently personal responsibility. Fourth, this separation allowed her to calm down, so that when she picked up Mark she didn't verbally lay into him. If she had bawled him out she probably would have ruined a wonderful learning opportunity. He would have projected his discomfort onto her in the form of anger and indignation. "What do you expect me to say? I screwed up, that's all! It's not like I robbed a bank or something. Look, just ground me or something, but don't preach to me like I'm some five-year-old!" By shaking her head in wonderment and not chastising him too harshly she forced him to stay responsible for what he had done.

After your teenager has committed an infraction, it is essential to communicate explicitly how, when, and for how long the consequence is in place. You both need to know at what point trust is restored to its previous level and when the breach is relegated to its proper place in history. For instance, it's unfair to tell teenagers that they can't use the car until you decide that they are ready, and then, when pressed, to say vaguely that somehow you'll know when they are once again ready. This will drive them crazy, and usually pushes them over the brink of irresponsibility to previously unimagined levels. Concrete steps and timelines help to contain their anxiety and invite them to be active on their own behalf in positive manners. Without this, most teenagers get overwhelmed and become passive—or worse, they act out in negative ways. Once the miscue takes place, sit down within twenty-four hours (or when everybody can think rationally once again) and negotiate the consequences. It is perfectly acceptable and wise not to have this discussion in the heat of the moment—a "we'll discuss where to go with this at lunch tomorrow" is often most appropriate. Also, as mentioned above, once a consequence is played out, it is unfair to resurrect it or the feelings associated with it in the future. The idea of the consequence is that it restores trust and allows everyone to move on. Holding history against one another is a prescription for a tumultuous relationship.

> I got in trouble for skipping class today and the vice principal called home already. So I'm sure my mom and dad are talking right now. By the time I get home they'll be so worked up that I'll have to stand trial for every single thing I've done wrong in the last ten years! You laugh, but it's true! Last time I got in trouble they re-lectured me about the time in fourth grade when I didn't lock my bike and it was stolen! That was when I blew up and fireworks began. What's a kid to do?

And of course, even when you don't hold history against your adolescent, it still may be their first line of defense, in spite of your best modeling. If you want to have a productive and useful discussion with your teenager, decline to engage in what therapists Ben Furman and Tapani Ahola call "reciprocal blaming."[2]

Ideally, before a consequence is enforced on an adolescent, there is input from both parties. As a parent you need to briefly state what the problem is and the general direction of the consequence (even if it appears your teenager has been awake most of the night worrying about this conversation).

> Just to quickly reiterate, we agreed that you would be in by midnight, and that in the event that you would be late you would give us a call so we wouldn't worry needlessly. But you didn't call and you came home an hour late. As I see it, you broke your agreement with us and cost each of us an hour's sleep—actually more, because we stayed up another hour after you got home, discussing what happened, but we won't pass that on to you as we accepted that possibility when we decided to become parents. So, any suggestions as to where we go from here?

The first few times you use this approach your kids probably won't have any suggestions, but over time they'll catch on and offer ideas of their own. Either way, you need to have thought through, without having attached yourself to, a plausible course of action.

> Well, let's deal with the lost time first, as that's the easier of the two issues. I was going to do laundry today and your father was going to mow the lawn, and since each task takes about an hour to complete, we suggest that you assume those responsibilities today so that we can have the time either to relax or to take a nap. Now, the broken agreement is a trickier matter. We suggest that for the next weekend your curfew gets moved back by one hour. At the end of next weekend we'll have a brief discussion and hopefully all

will go back to normal. If, however, something else happens, we'll sit down and start all over again. So, what do you say? Any questions or changes you want to suggest? OK, then let's let this be the end of it.

Note that the consequences discussion is definitely not the time to lecture or explain how the transgression affected you. (The pull to have the guilt-inducing conversation is usually quite powerful at this point. Resist. Guilt-inducement only sabotages any potential lesson.) Your teenager knows quite well how those actions affected you. In fact, your explanation will probably only make things worse from her perspective: she now feels talked down to in a manner that, for her, simply rubs it in. As for the lesson, well, she'll connect the dots in private, away from you. This is part of her developing sense of independence and personal responsibility.

When teenagers talk about their parents, they often mention "parental lectures" or the "parental units in lecture mode." It seems that every kid can rattle off six or seven of their parents' most oft-repeated teaching stories. A psychologist I know uses the following exercise to make this point.

> A mother and her teenage daughter came into the psychologist's office. The girl didn't feel like she had any problems, but her mother was sure that she had a few. So the psychologist spoke first with the daughter alone, then with the mother alone, and then with both of them together. At the next meeting the psychologist first met with the daughter alone and asked her about the repetitive lectures from her mother that she had mentioned in their first meeting. She asked how well she knew them. The girl assured her that she knew them quite well. Well enough to repeat them for her and a tape recorder, the psychologist asked? The girl smiled and said yes. With that the girl recorded two of her mother's most "favorite" lectures. Later on in the session the tape was played for the mother as a means of showing her that what she said to her daughter was indeed registering, even though she didn't necessarily show it. In fact, it

quickly became obvious that since the "teaching" intentions of the talks had long since been accomplished, they were now only distancing and demeaning! It was clear to the mother that her daughter had gotten her messages; all she could hope for now was that during moments of decision-making, her words would receive some attention before she acted. Also, the mom realized that her words aren't necessarily sufficient for her daughter to learn from. She had to learn her own lessons.

Some final points about natural consequences. Obviously, understanding the law of cause and effect is the purpose behind using natural consequences. But be careful that an understanding of these laws doesn't let the adolescent off the hook; make sure he has to deal with the consequences in the action of his life. Otherwise you inadvertently encourage the notion that understanding and remorse is enough, and therefore sidestep the learning that will positively affect behavior.

> Whenever I get in any trouble I hardly ever get punished. At first my parents take turns yelling at me, which really pisses me off, but I sit there and take it for the most part. Then, just before the punishment part of the conversation, I take over with some sort of apology, a few tears, and a promise to never do anything like that again. After awhile, once that they see that I truly understand and that I'm sorry, they just forget about it. And it's not like I do this stuff to just get off the hook. I actually do feel bad and sorry for what I did. I guess I'm just really good at being sorry.

It is also important to take your time in determining consequences; otherwise you'll overreact and then have to go back on what you said. For instance, to ground your teenager for coming home late is one thing, but in the heat of the moment to extend the punishment to six months is another. This is something you will not, should not, or cannot follow through on. Still, when it does happen and you do overreact, don't be afraid to apologize later on, maybe even taking back some of what you said. That kind of honesty is more useful than any lecture, as long as it is sincere.

Personal influence is also quite important during this process. Over time teenagers will learn that while they must face the consequences of their actions, they can also influence the course and creativity of the consequences. Thus, the door is opened to realistic negotiation and compromise on the front end of parent-adolescent agreements. Most parents would be amazed at how many times kids make an agreement knowing that they won't stick to it and knowing that they'll be caught breaking the agreement. They do this because they don't feel they have any influence on the front end. If there is no room for sincere negotiation, they discover that the best course of action is to agree to anything and get on with their business.

> Half the reason I lie is because my mother doesn't really give me any choice. She keeps herself so naive and idealistic that I can't be honest with her. If I were honest then she wouldn't let me do anything; I would spend every weekend night watching movies with my parents! I wish she could handle my honesty without freaking out, and let me run my life. If she trusted me more, I would trust her more. Like the parties I go to. Her rule is that I can't go to any party where there is alcohol, even though I don't drink. That rules out most of the parties. So I usually lie about the alcohol or where I'm going. But like the other night somebody got really drunk and it was scary. Normally I would talk to my mom about something like that, but because I have to lie to her I can't talk to her about what happened. And that's too bad for both of us.

This brings us to the topic of grounding, a consequence that is rife with difficulties. If thought through and followed through responsibly and reasonably, it can be an excellent consequence. But grounding is seldom enacted in this manner. Typically, grounding is the consequence of choice in the heat of the moment when a parent wants to witness the effects of the punishment on their teenager. Unfortunately, all this does is escalate the tension, anxiety, and general bad feelings. Moreover, the grounding consequence is seldom fully enforced, and teenagers know this. When pressed about the grounding consequence at home, most adolescents say they know their parents are acting in the heat of the moment. For one teenager, a one-month grounding typically translates into one week. For another, getting grounded for three weeks translates into being good for a few days with the certainty that her parents will forget about the grounding by the weekend. When pressed even further, kids acknowledge the dance aspect to the whole grounding ritual. This is where they get upset, angry, apologetic, or sullen in order to let their parents know the punishment got to them, but these emotions often mean the loss of the battle (showing the effects of the supposed grounding) in favor of the victory of the war (able to go out again by the next weekend).

But realize that grounding is usually ineffective, because most parents forget that when they ground their teenager they also ground themselves. At least that is how it should be. Kids are grounded for breaking some sort of rule or agreement; they are guilty of at least a momentary inability to monitor their own behavior. They cannot, therefore, oversee their own grounding. Rather, they need assistance in self-monitoring so that they are able to reflect and learn from their error; otherwise it will just happen again. They need more, not less, structure. And who better than parents to provide such structure. When parents ground their kids they are also grounding themselves, because they must provide the temporarily increased structure (supervision) for their adolescent. For example, when a child is learning to ride a bike and he continually falls down, the responsible parent provides both the training wheels (the grounding) and the sensitive supervision (their presence). The same must be true when grounding a teenager.

Two more points on grounding. First is that the purpose of grounding is for teenagers to learn that their actions do indeed have consequences, and that they must face them. This becomes evident when kids accept their consequences without a struggle. In some way they have considered the long-term consequences and opted in favor of the short-term gain, and along the way acknowledged to themselves that they'll deal with and accept the consequences later. A teacher once told me about this incident, which is quite illustrative.

The other day a student skipped my class and missed a pop quiz. What is different about this story is that she found me early the next day to let me know that she was aware that she skipped my class. She wanted to make sure that I knew that it was nothing personal and that something else had required her immediate attention. Furthermore, in her mind, it was worth the consequences she would face for skipping my class. When I informed her that we had a pop quiz she gulped and acknowledged that she knew my policy on skipped classes: a zero for the day, including tests and homework, with no opportunity for make-up. She then shocked me by saying that was fair, even though she didn't like it, and that she understood it! Without divulging the details, I made sure that the next time I had contact with her parents I let them know what a responsible daughter they had and complimented them on whatever it was they were doing that allowed this responsibility to come to such fruition.

Second, grounding can also present a rare opportunity for the family to reconnect with one another. Because of the nature of the teenage world, often the only way to ask for something is to do the opposite. The following is not an unusual a story.

A father came up to me after a presentation to support the idea of multiple meanings of some behaviors. In this instance his son had clearly violated their curfew agreement, which was unusual for this child. The parents ended up grounding him for the next night, which was Saturday. To be responsible they also canceled their Saturday evening plans. The early part of the evening was awkward, as they all hadn't been home on a Saturday night in a long time. After dinner they dispersed into their usual evening patterns until about 9:00 p.m., when the son suggested they rent a movie. Since he was grounded one of his parents made the trip and the choice. Well, to make a long story short, they ended up watching the movie, eating popcorn, and then talking for quite awhile after the movie—about nothing important, just talking. At the end of the night the dad told his son that he better be careful, as he liked the way this grounding had turned out, and that he might have to use it more often!

Grounding is an effective consequence when it is thought through and when used for a short duration. However, it is not meant to substitute for responsible parenting; in fact, it demands more parental attention than other consequences.

To this point, natural consequences have been viewed from the perspective of parents toward adolescents, but the same principles hold true from the perspective of becoming better parents. You learn how to be a better parent through the natural consequences of your actions, non-actions, words, and periods of silence with your teenager. If you are open to your kids, and can discriminate between useful and unproductive feedback, they will teach you quite a bit about parenting, and about yourself.

> It's embarrassing to admit, but there are certainly times when my daughter is right about some of the inappropriate stances I take in some of our disagreements. In particular she is adept at catching me in the "power trip," where I demand her to do or not do something simply because I am the parent. Usually it has her best interests at heart, but other times it is simply to assert my authority. When she is on, she is the clearest mirror around—one that's sometimes difficult to look into.

Endnotes

1. *Children the Challenge*, by Rudolf Dreikurs, offers an excellent commentary on the role of natural consequences in the disciplining of children.

2. Furman, Ben and Tapani Ahola, *Solution Talk: Hosting Therapeutic Conversations*.

CHAPTER 7

Alcohol, Drugs, and Parties

*I'm concerned about my tenth grader going
to weekend parties where alcohol and drugs are
available. What can or should I do about it?*

Many parents worry about the influence of alcohol and drugs on their adolescent's development, and specifically that the complications of "normal" teenage behavior are escalated when drugs or alcohol are factors: a drunk-driving arrest, an accident while under the influence, or a sexual compromise—just to name a few possible disasters. These fears are legitimate, especially considering the risk-taking nature of adolescents. To address these issues, some means of reflection and information are in order.

Some readers will find this a frightening chapter to read because the reality is harsh and difficult to face. But try to make the leap of sympathy necessary to grasp the following information, which is vital to your understanding your teenager's world.

To begin with, take some time to reflect on the following questions. Answer them honestly and separate from your role as a parent. Then keep your reflections in mind for the rest of this discussion.

Think back to your high school and post-high school years.[1]

- ◆ What kind of kid were you?
- ◆ Who were your friends?
- ◆ What was your family like?
- ◆ What did you do for fun? In school? On weekends?

- Did you do things behind your parents' backs? Like what? Why?

- How did these activities affect your development as a person? What was harmful? Helpful?

- Would your parents have been upset to catch you doing these things?

- How did they respond if they did catch you? Was it a helpful response? Why or why not?

- From an adult perspective, were you ever at risk or truly in danger? Did you feel the same back then?

- Is there anything anyone in particular could have said or done to influence your behaviors, even in some minor way?

In part, teenagers experiment with alcohol and drugs because they are readily available in their day-to-day lives. There is virtually nothing that parents can do about this. As frightening as it sounds, alcohol and drugs are accessible to kids beginning in middle school. By the time they reach high school accessibility isn't an issue; only desire is. What parents can do is educate themselves, model a healthy relationship with alcohol, provide clear guidelines, expectations, and consequences, and always emphasize safety as the bottom line. These are the directions we need to explore in addressing this topic. First, what draws adolescents toward drug and alcohol experimentation? Much of the attraction proceeds naturally from the issues examined in the Chapter 2. Three horizons identified in that chapter play an integral role: social, friendship, and personal identity.

Socially, experimenting with drinking or drugs creates an immediate niche for the teenager. At a time when fitting in is crucial, drugs and alcohol temporarily resolve questions of acceptance. That is, by using drugs or alcohol they often experience an easy acceptance into a group of peers (usually desirable peers in their eyes), *and* consequently slip into a ready-made social life. Now, there are choices of what to do on weekends, and "friends" are probably calling and including them in on their plans. Also, adolescents' defenses are lowered under the influence of alcohol or drugs—they are less self-conscious and more spontaneous, two highly desirable traits.

I was never all that sure of myself with friends. It seemed like I really wasn't close to anybody, at least not in the way I wanted. But when I started partying a little bit, all of a sudden I loosened up. I was more confident and liked myself more. And most important, people seemed to really like me. They said I was funny and lively. And soon I had a full social life. Lots of phone calls during the week and invitations to parties on the weekends. It was terrific!

Adolescents feels an initial sense of intimacy when accepted into a social group—especially if they have been longing for social acceptance into a group of friends. They feel the pseudo-intimacy one develops while using alcohol and drugs—especially if one is relatively inexperienced. In this new social group and while under the influence, they are probably experiencing their most open conversations, which are often felt as real intimacy. Their defenses are down and they are reveling in sharing their "true self" and having others do the same. In a sense, they briefly escape their singular identity and somewhat merge with another. The hitch is that while the closeness may be real, the means are artificial (which, of course, is an idea that most parents live by and that most teenagers are unable to comprehend). They haven't yet developed the necessary skills or addressed their fundamental aloneness to achieve true intimacy. They haven't earned it; instead, they have artificially made the leap, which in too many instances leaves them dependent on the artificial means. Or, as veterans of the sixties recall:

When I took drugs I saw God!

What did God say to you?

Don't take drugs.

By partially defining themselves through alcohol and drug use, teenagers are also distancing themselves from their parents, since few parents encourage the use of alcohol or drugs in their adolescent's lives. In this sense, the choice to go against parental guidelines is an assertion of independence and autonomy. They feel more in charge of their lives. We've seen that asserting independence and developing a stable personal identity are crucial for eventual transition into the adult world. However, when alcohol and drugs are the central means, there is cause for concern, besides the obvious health and safety issues.

For many adolescents, alcohol and drugs are a means of covering up or keeping unconscious certain developmental issues and personal conflicts that are only resolvable on a conscious level. They relegate these conflicts to the unconscious realm to be routinely "acted out," without ever consciously addressing them. Unfortunately, we have all seen adults stuck in this pattern when they abuse alcohol and drugs. Such people often exhibit significant personality changes while under the influence, such as withdrawal, depression, outrageously extroverted behavior, or aggression. Alcohol or drug abuse relieves the internal stress and pressure brought on by unconscious conflicts without ever addressing the ongoing source of stress. An extreme example:

> I started getting high daily just as my parents started fighting more [they eventually got divorced]. It was really crazy in my house at that time, so I would come home, go up to my room, and get high pretty much every day. Sometimes I even got stoned in the morning while walking to school. It was all just too crazy. But it was the only way I could cope.

And a not-so-extreme example:

> Yeah, I pretty much party every weekend, but it's no big deal. I mean it's the only time I get to relax and kick back. The rest of the time there is so much pressure to get good grades, succeed, practice hard, and be a good person. This [partying] is my time, when I can just forget about all the expectations, goals, and guilt, and just let go and be myself.

You may be thinking that alcohol and drug experimentation is a terrible thing. However, in real life it is not this cut-and-dried. Many teenagers are able to experiment with drugs and alcohol without becoming dependent, and in a manner that doesn't impede their ability to grow and mature. Recent research by Jonathon Shedler and Jack Block[2] showed that adolescents who experimented moderately with drugs (no more than one time per month and usually just marijuana) were psychologically healthier than those who abused drugs (more than one time per month), *and* than those who abstained from drugs altogether. This is not to say that drug experimentation is either good or recommended; rather, it indicates that drug abuses are the symptoms of deeper problems (or, as we'll discuss later, frequently the result of a biological or genetic predisposition). In this study, which followed the same 101 boys and girls over fifteen years, those who were psychologically the healthiest as children were the same ones who just moderately experimented with drugs as teenagers. This, I believe, puts drug experimentation into a more differentiated framework. While moderate experimentation is not necessarily good, it is also not necessarily a sign of a deep psychological crisis. On the other hand, more than casual experimentation is cause for deep concern, not only as a problem in itself, but also as a sign of deeper problems. This research clearly shows that drug or alcohol use can itself be the cover to deeper issues.

In summary, the initial acceptance into a social group that comes with using alcohol and drugs is provisional, as many teenagers (and adults) discover when they try to drop the use and keep the same social group. Adolescents—and, again, adults—crave intimate discussions, but shouldn't have to be under the influence to be intimate. And, as the reliance on alcohol or drugs for intimacy grows, the skills for true intimacy atrophy. Differentiating yourself from those around you in a way that is true to yourself is a necessarily long and at times arduous process—there are no shortcuts, including alcohol and drug use.

Before we discuss what parents can do, let's go over some basic information on alcohol and a variety of available drugs. Alcohol is familiar: most of us go to parties and functions where alcohol is served regularly. We have all developed our own personal relationships with alcohol—possibly punctuated by a few painful lessons along the way. Alcohol is a part of the adult world in this country; adolescents using alcohol are prematurely acting like adults. Drugs are a slightly different matter. They are illegal and fewer adults have experienced them. To many, they are a frightening mystery. At this point, a piece of advice: If you don't know the differences between various drugs (and you probably won't because they are changeable and cyclical to a very high degree), then educate yourself. Try your local library or bookstore (also see the Bibliography in this book.). It is both naive and blinding to link all drugs in the same category. What follows is a very brief description of a few of the more available drugs.[3, 4]

> *Marijuana (Cannabis)*: A plant that is typically smoked. The psychoactive ingredient is tetrahydrocannabinol (THC), which has dramatically increased in concentration from the 1960s to the present, and is at least five to seven times more potent. "Marijuana can act as a stimulant or depressant depending on the variety and amount of chemical that is absorbed in the brain, but most often, it acts as a relaxant, making users sleepy, drowsy, and more inner focused." The effects last from four to six hours and begin to affect the user within twenty minutes of smoking.

> *Cocaine*: Comes from the coca plant. In its powder form this drug is most often snorted, and is absorbed into the brain within three to five minutes. The subjective effect of cocaine is very pleasurable: "increased confidence, a willingness to work (sometimes endlessly), a diminishing of life's problems, and a euphoric rush." The drug is metabolized quickly by the body, typically within forty minutes, so the effects are relatively short-lived. Physically there is a significant increase in the release of epinephrine [adrenalin] that "raises the blood pressure, increases the heart rate, causes rapid breathing, tenses muscles, and causes the jitters."

> *Crack Cocaine*: A chemically altered form of cocaine that is smokeable. It is cheaper than cocaine with the same effects, except that it is much more intense and is absorbed much more quickly into the brain, generally five to eight seconds.

> *Amphetamines (Speed)*: A stimulant that is usually ingested orally, but that can be snorted, smoked, or injected. Amphetamines have cocaine-like effects but of longer duration and at a significantly lower cost. Amphetamines come in a variety of forms and strengths.

> *LSD*: A psychedelic that "can cause mental changes and psychedelic effects," depending on the dose, which is seldom

known by the typical street purchaser. LSD directly affects the emotional center of the brain and thus opens the user to euphoria and/or panic. Thus the user's mental set and the setting of the experience contribute significantly to the effects of the drug. Discernable effects from the drug last eight to twelve hours. Typical doses of LSD are smaller than those taken during the sixties, thus making the effect similar to amphetamines. If a high school student is under the influence of drugs during school, this is probably the drug of choice.

"Designer Drugs" (MDA, MMDA, MDM, MDE): Synthetic drugs that create feelings of euphoria, intimacy, and well-being. They derive from the amphetamine molecule and thus also induce stimulatory effects. Each varies in duration, but in general lasts eight to twelve hours.

Heroin: Part of the opiate family that when injected directly into the bloodstream takes fifteen to thirty seconds to affect the central nervous system. Subjectively, the user experiences intense and extreme euphoria.

Alcohol: The oldest psychoactive drug known to man that, when used in moderation, reduces inhibitions and lessens tension. "The more alcohol that is drunk the freer the user feels but the blood pressure is lowered, motor reflexes are slowed, digestion becomes poor, body heat is lost, and sexual excitement is diminished." Different types of alcohol vary in strength depending on the "proof" (100 percent alcohol = 200 proof). Generally, beer is 4 percent to 8 percent, wine is 12 percent, and liquors are 40 percent to 43 percent.

So, how do people go from occasional use to addiction? The most common theory of addiction includes components of biology, psychology, and sociology. Some of these statistics are frightening:[5]

- ◆ If one parent is an alcoholic or addict, the child is 34 percent more likely to suffer from some sort of addiction.

- ◆ If both parents are alcoholics or addicts, their child is 400 percent more likely to suffer from some sort of addiction.

◆ If a person is male and both his father and grandfather are alcoholics or addicts, he is 900 percent more likely to suffer from some sort of addiction.

Scientists have been able to breed pure "wino" and pure "teetotaller" mice in laboratories. The mice are alike in every manner other than their drinking preferences. Further, by either forcing the teetotallers to drink or inflicting significant amounts of stress on them (which in turn leads them to drink), researchers see the brain chemistry of the teetotallers change to that of the winos. Thus, it appears that stress and forced consumption can alter a person's brain chemistry from non-alcoholic to alcoholic.

The graph below illustrates the path that addiction follows along the compulsion curve in an individual. Two points are important to keep in mind. First, biological predisposition determines how quickly one moves along this curve. That is, a highly sensitive person moves from experimental use to abuse after only several exposures (Abuse used here means the continued use of drugs or alcohol in spite of the negative consequences it causes in one's life). A person not predisposed to addiction may take years to move along the curve to abuse. Second, once a person goes past habituation there is no turning back; abstinence must be practiced in order to stay sober. Prior to that point, an individual can move back along the curve to social or experimental use.

Diagram 2: Compulsion Curve

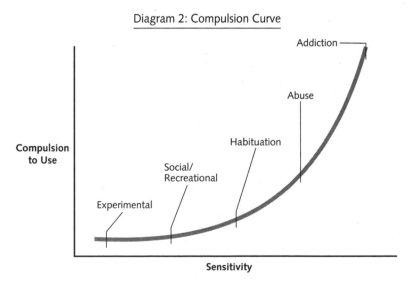

Now to the question of who becomes alcoholics and addicts. As Dr. Inaba is fond of saying: "contrary to popular belief, it is not exclusively the bad, stupid, amoral, or disenfranchised. It is actually quite the opposite; most addicts or alcoholics fall into the categories of educated, intelligent, skilled, and sensitive." For instance, physicians are eight times more likely to become addicts than members of the general population, and six times more likely to be alcoholics. Also, those with the highest rate of addiction and alcoholism belong to the group MENSA, whose members must have an IQ of 140 and a personal recommendation just to take the entrance exam. Thus, and painfully ironic, adolescents that are bright, motivated, and ambitious are actually in the highest-risk category. Finally, remember that the preceding is only a general background on alcohol, drug, and addiction theory.

Back to the initial question of what parents can do. The answer is both a lot and not much. Short of keeping your teenager in the house every night, there is nothing you can do to guarantee that she will not drink or use drugs. Not very practical. Checking her breath at night (or in extreme circumstances, urine samples), also doesn't do much to prevent the behavior. Neither parents nor anyone else can prevent drinking or drug use, but it does not mean that all is hopeless. Far from it.

Perhaps the most crucial factors are the conversations you have with your adolescent *before* usage ever becomes an issue and the example you set in your relationship to alcohol and drugs. Adolescents look and test for congruency. In your conversations on this topic, clearly outline your position on alcohol and drugs; acknowledge the reality of the adolescent world; and discuss possible consequences of broken agreements, like time-limited grounding, car restrictions, and earlier curfews. Again, let the consequences speak for themselves so that drug and alcohol use doesn't turn into a power struggle later. Then expect her to mess up, or at least don't be surprised if it happens. And—here is the tricky part—without becoming adversarial or hyper-suspicious, you must catch her when she break the rules. This is the structure you've established for her to experiment within, should she decide to experiment. If she does experiment, then she will gauge her behavior according to this structure and will monitor herself enough to escape detection. This greatly reduces the risk of catastrophic accidents and destructive habits. And be savvy; when she says it was the first time she experimented, give her ample time to reconsider and be very suspicious if she sticks to the "first time" story. Believe it or not, it's fairly simple to escape detection if one is very careful and conscientious, so if you catch her, she is getting sloppy in her precautions (a bad sign). If, however, you keep your eyes closed, you essentially relax the structure and create room for more out-of-control and potentially catastrophic behavior.

> At first when I began to party, I was real careful not to get caught. I always stopped [partying] a couple of hours before going home, ate some smelly food, and sometimes even changed my clothes if there had been a lot of smoking going on. It was a hassle and all, but at least I was pretty sure I wouldn't get caught. But after awhile I began to realize that my parents didn't have a clue! It got to the point where I began to wonder what it would take to get caught. I remember once even finishing a beer on the back porch before heading into bed. I even said goodnight to my dad! Another time I was so wasted that I never got past the living room sofa, where I passed out for the night. In the morning they [parents] asked me why I slept on the sofa. I told them I wasn't tired when I got home so I watched some TV and must have fallen asleep. They believed me without a second thought, even though the TV was off and I was facing the wrong direction on the sofa!

On the other hand:

> I swear my dad has a bloodhound's nose. If I even have a sip of beer or one smoke he smells it on me from ten feet away! And since I have to wake my parents when I get home to say good night there is no way I can get away with it. It isn't worth lying about, so I usually cop to it and deal with the consequences. At least it's all on the table that way.

Now, how to handle the parties. Make your expectations clear to your teenager, as well as your own role. For instance, if the rule is no unchaperoned parties and you insist that your son provide you with the parents' address and phone number, you must be consistent in acquiring this information. (Expect him to test you, and if you forget once, expect him to express shock and indignation when you next ask for the information.) Then, by all means, get through your own discomfort and shyness and call the parents, if that was the agreement. Otherwise, you'll make it too seductive for him to lie at a future date. If he must follow the agreed-upon rules, then you must enforce them.

> Part of the problem is that it is really, really easy to lie to my parents. Too easy. They set all these standards and agreements but they never follow through, so I just tell them what they want to hear and go about my business.

Also, you may turn out to be the only parent who phones the chaperone, which may delight them if they had planned on being out of town that night! Which leads to a very important point on the whole topic of raising adolescents. High school students live in a very tight community. For the most part they all know or know of one another in their school. They understand the norms of their high school culture, including the various social scenes. On the other hand, most parents have minimal contact with their kids' school culture, and tend to rely on off-hand comments by their teenager, their friends, or the media, none of which is very reliable. Parents often live in relative ignorance about their kids' lives, and frankly, most kids like it this way. So if you want to be informed, you need to make it happen. Don't be afraid to call the chaperone of any party your teenager wants to attend. And go to school events, even if just to meet other parents. As long as your presence isn't too conspicuous, your teenager may act one way and silently feel somewhat differently.

> I used to be real embarrassed that my dad came to every soccer game I played. He was always there from start to finish; always wished me good luck beforehand and always said "good game" after each game. It was sort of a pain, even if it was sort of cute, too. Anyway, he unexpectedly missed a game this year. What was surprising was that I missed having him there. When I got home I asked him where he

was today, and he said that he had forgotten! I couldn't believe it. I was so mad even though I didn't say anything.

Back to the parties. As in other areas of the parent-adolescent relationship, a useful perspective from which to develop party-going guidelines is the future. Imagine when your teenager is leaving home for college or to move into her first apartment. At this point she is essentially on her own with no direct supervision or guidelines other than the law—and the experience she's had with your structure during high school. So, when she leaves home, with what continuum of experiences and decisions must she be familiar in order to successfully handle this level of freedom?

> We talked with Karen regularly between ninth and twelfth grades about party guidelines. Essentially we had a system of increased freedom and responsibility that developed out of negotiation and her behavior relative to the guidelines. It started in the ninth grade, when she couldn't go to any unchaperoned parties, and increased in freedom until second-semester senior year, when she made decisions on which parties to attend and was responsible for being home at a reasonable time without any explicit curfew. Overall it worked quite well. Sure, there were a few rough and doubtful moments along the way, but oddly enough there were no problems during the end of the senior year, when we most expected difficulties. In fact, by then she was talking to us more openly than ever.

Be willing, too, to periodically play the "fall guy" for your teenager. Even if it's a stretch of the truth, you can do things that allow your adolescent to gracefully say no.

> I had gotten drunk a few times at parties with my friends, but I didn't like it too much. At the same time, though, I wanted to fit in. Finally one night I couldn't take it anymore, so I blurted it all out to my dad. After he got over the initial shock he kind of smiled to himself and asked if I wanted some help. A couple of weeks later I went to a party and had a couple of beers (as my dad and I had planned). When my

friends dropped me off he was waiting up for me. Needless to say everyone knew I was in big trouble! And as pre-arranged, he yelled a little (just loud enough for them to hear) and I got "grounded" for a week. Of course I complained bitterly to my friends, but from then on they completely understood when I didn't want to drink anymore.

Finally, health and safety are the bottom line. No matter what poor decisions have been made, what rules have been violated, or what lies have been told, teenagers must know deep in the marrow of their bones that their overall safety far outweighs all other concerns.

At the very beginning of high school, my parents sat me down for our "alcohol talk." Nothing unusual there, except at the end. My father leaned forward and said, "Now, no matter what happens, understand that your safety is more important to us than any of these rules. So, in the unlikely but possible event that you are in a position where you are unable to safely get home—you've been drinking, the driver has been drinking, or whatever comes up—you must promise to call us, anytime, day or night. We'll come get you, and we won't ask any questions or ever report your friends. In the morning we will talk about it, but understand that when you show that level of responsibility the consequences will be minimal. No matter what else we've said tonight, this is by far the most important. Do you understand?" Since then, I have had to call a few times, and each time it has worked out fairly well.

In this same health-and-safety discussion (and in the driver's-license discussion) it's a good idea to talk about the role of the designated driver. Fortunately, this is a role that more and more teenagers are taking seriously. It's also a great way for adolescents to be a part of the group without having to get into drug or alcohol use.

More teenagers use designated drivers than most people think. I know most of my friends do. At most parties, there are actually *two* parties going on—the larger one with alcohol, and a smaller one for the designated drivers who are drinking soda.

I recently called the home of a friend who has a seventeen-year-old daughter. Clearly she had gotten the message about alcohol and drug use. Nobody was home and I got her voice on the answering machine:

> Hello, nobody is home now so please leave a message after the tone. If this is you, Mom, I'm at Theresa's house, or I'm out smoking and drinking.

As I'm sure you've noticed, as with the previous chapter on structure and limits, there is no ideal, no right set of rules and guidelines for alcohol and drug experimentation. Each family is different and must develop their own. What is essential is that the guidelines are consistent with other family values and beliefs, and that everyone follow through on the agreements they make. This is how trust is developed.

Endnotes

1. The post-high school years are included here for adults, because with the increasing pace of social change, your kids are facing certain issues and decisions much earlier than you did.

2. Shedler, Jonathan and Block, Jack, "Adolescent Drug Use and Psychological Health: A Longitudinal Inquiry," Volume 45, Number 5.

3. As drugs and drug potencies are constantly changing, the information that follows is almost or is already somewhat out-of-date. Use this data as background information only.

4. The information that follows is excerpted from a book that I highly recommend by Darryl S. Inaba, Pharm. D. and William E. Cohen, *Uppers, Downers, and All Arounders.*

5. These statistics are quoted from a talk given by Dr. Darryl Inaba to the parents and faculty of University High School in February 1994.

❧ CHAPTER 8 ❧

Academics, Grades, and Motivation

What can I do to keep my kids motivated in school and working toward good grades?

First, a few general comments about grades. For many parents and teenagers, grades are a source of conflict. This conflict is far from simple because grades take on so many different meanings in the typical adolescent's life.

Melinda, a high school student, is an example of how complicated the issue gets when her dad asks how she did on a recent history test. For now, assume that Melinda is doing fairly well with her grades. When her dad asks about the history test, these thoughts go through her head, but at such a rapid rate that few are articulate even to her.

- ◆ Cool, great that he remembered, what a great dad!

- ◆ I'm glad he asked because now I can tell him how well I'm doing and maybe he'll give me some more space or extra allowance, but if I tell him how well I did I know I'll get that smug "I told you so" look! He'll think it was because he told me to get off the phone early last night, even though it wasn't (and I can't tell him that I snuck the extension into the bathroom and talked for two more hours!)

- ◆ If I tell him now, he'll always expect an answer; then when I do poorly, he'll know because I won't answer. So maybe I shouldn't answer at all.

- Amazing that he remembers to ask about my history test but he never remembers what time I have to be picked up after practice.

- History test, what history test? Oh God, was that today! It seems so long ago; I mean, so much has happened today. How can he expect me to talk about that history test compared to everything else that has happened?

- Can't he just trust me a little bit; I mean, why does he have to check up on me all the time?

Whatever mix of thoughts go through Melinda's head, a minimal response is often the result: "Uh, OK I guess. What's for dinner tonight?" Any other response, from Melinda's point of view, is too complicated and cumbersome to get into.

Unfortunately, our current education system takes grades as a literal indicator of a student's success. Most students study for the grade first and for the knowledge and education second. This gets the entire educational process off on the wrong foot. Grades reflect only an aspect of a student's intellectual development, and an even smaller portion of their development as people. Kids ought be in school for the sake of learning, not simply for getting grades; and parents play an essential role here. Over the long run, parents pay dearly for driving their kids to study solely for the sake of grades. But what are the alternatives?

When most parents ask their teenager how she is doing in geometry, they are really asking about the grade (at least, that is what it feels like to the adolescent, regardless of the parent's intent). And when parents ask how their teenager did on a history test, they are really asking about the grade (again, this is what it sounds like from the adolescent's perspective). From the parents' point of view, they make such inquiries because one, they grew up with and understand this system, and two, asking about grades is often the only way they know to show interest in and monitor their adolescent's studies. But if you wish to instill learning and education as a lifelong and enjoyable process for your teenager, consider these new lines of inquiry:

- Ask Melinda what she is finding challenging as well as boring in her history class.

- ♦ Ask Melinda if she has had any particularly difficult math problems lately that she has surprised herself by being able to figure out.

- ♦ Ask her how she managed to hang in there long enough to figure out the problem, rather than giving up on herself.

- ♦ Ask her what kind of questions she is asking about *Jane Eyre* in her English class.

- ♦ Ask her where she is getting her ideas for painting.

- ♦ Ask if the history test was a good test: did it help her to understand the material at a deeper level, or was it simply a check to make sure she was doing the reading?

These questions inquire about the process of learning—the actual fabric of learning in all its nuances and subtleties—without ever focusing on grades. This type of questioning is the only type that makes sense if you want to turn your child onto learning. Once kids get excited and curious about learning, everything else will more or less fall into place, even motivation and grades. However, if grades are the focus for you, then you are inadvertently supporting certain undesirable behaviors, including cheating. With an overemphasis on grades, it makes a great deal of sense to a teenager to figure out ways to cheat—read, "to get the best possible grades."

Recall an academic experience of which you are fond. What comes to mind first: the grade or something about the process of how you got through the experience? The fact that I completed a dissertation and that my committee liked it takes a distant second place to the satisfaction I had in knowing I had hung in there when things were ambiguous and seemingly at a dead end. Nor could the passing grade I got hold a candle to how I knew the process had changed my way of thinking and my perspective of the topic as well as of my own person. Yet very few people know how to ask about this stuff. Go ahead, learn and practice on your teenager. They might be confused at first, but they'll catch on quickly. And who knows, with time they might even come to enjoy it. Further, this kind of dialogue feels much less judgmental to adolescents than talking about grades.

Finally, the single most influential thing you can do to support learning is to practice what you preach. Set aside family time in the evening for study and reading. Kids do homework and parents read or work quietly. Sure, some parents say that they've worked all day, so they need to relax at home—but kids have worked all day, too. If you sit down in front of the television for a few hours and yell at your kids to go study, you're sending a mixed message: "I say that learning is important but I don't act that way." (See Chapter 11 for more on this subject.)

Q: What can I do to help my teenager improve his poor grades?

In my mind, this is a case of natural consequences doing the work (anything else is probably at least inefficient and uncomfortable). Nagging your adolescent about homework is an unenviable task, and it usually doesn't work! I have had the following conversation countless times with teenagers (and their success as students is an irrelevant variable):

> *Me:* So, what exactly happens when you sit down to do your homework?
>
> *Student:* Well, after talking to a friend or two on the phone and procrastinating for awhile I finally sit down and begin working. And I usually can get into it and get a lot done if I'm left alone! But that hardly ever happens. My brother wants to show me something in his room, or the TV is on loud and gets my attention. But even these aren't too bad; I mean I can get it back together after that.
>
> *Me:* Then what's the problem?
>
> *Student:* The problem is when my parents constantly check in on me and treat me like a little kid! I'll be reading or something and my mom will stick her head in (without knocking!), look at me and say, "Oh, I just wanted to see if you were still working." By the time she closes the door behind her I've lost it. I mean, what am I, ten or something?

At that point I throw the book down in disgust and usually never open it again that night.

Me: Have you ever talked to her about this?

Student: I've tried, but all that happens is that she gets more slippery in how she checks in.

Me: What do you mean?

Student: Well, instead of directly asking about my homework she finds some excuse to talk to me: "Any dirty dishes in here?" or "Do you have a game tomorrow?" or "Do you want me to wake you in the morning?" But like the whole time she is staring at what book I'm reading and what is on my desk. It's just too obvious!

Me: Hmm, any chance she really is legitimate in what she is asking?

Student: Sure, but it's the way she does it and when she does it that gets to me. It's so transparent.

Essentially, school is your teenager's job, a job that has clear parameters and expectations. Have this conversation with your adolescent—usually sometime during freshmen or sophomore year. Include what is important to you, and ask what he thinks needs modification. Then ask him what role he wants you to play; expect a surprised look followed by, "Uh, what do you mean?" Then have a few options laid out to appeal to his creativity: "Well, we could agree to a specific homework time and we (Mom and Dad) could remind you of it when you forget and periodically checkup on you so you don't get distracted. Or we could go over each homework assignment with you to see how well you've done on each one. Or we could..." Eventually, you want him to assume honest responsibility for his homework and ask for your help periodically, though you might have regular, agreed-upon check-ins (once every week or two) to see how things are going. Build a means of support that allows you to feel active and that actually does support your adolescent. This is easier to say than do, but it can be done with some patience and persistence, as I learned in a different context a few years ago.

When my wife was completing her Master's thesis in Architecture, I was a very well-intentioned pain in the neck. In an effort to be supportive, I asked her every day how the writing was going. What she had worked on today? Did she want me to read anything for feedback? Well, my queries were hardly ever received in the manner intended. Typically, she abruptly ended the conversation in a huff, leaving me shaking my head. Why didn't she want my help and support? In fact, she said she preferred that I not ask her about her writing at all! I couldn't stand the idea of being that passive, nor could she handle my constant pacing back and forth. Then one day she hit on the solution. It was brilliant. She said, "Michael, I know that you love me and only want to help, but your constant questions on my progress are distracting and irritating. At the same time, I don't want to push you away. So I have an idea of how you can help me. Anytime you want to support or assist me, the best thing you can say is: 'Work hard and work well.' Nothing else. That's it! That is what I need the most from you, your quiet support and faith." It worked wonderfully. I felt there was something I could do, and she felt supported.

In a similar vein, a parent once reported the following to me:

> My husband and I recently realized just how much we nag our daughter Karen about her homework. But to not do or say anything feels terrible. So finally we talked with her about our dilemma. We wanted her to help us with a solution. After just a few minutes (once she understood that we were sincere, and how much she stood to gain) she came up with a great idea. At around 9:30 each night, one of us would knock on her door and get her "order" for the night. We would then make her the tea of her choice and bring it to her in her room along with three cups. We would then drink tea together and chat lightly, sometimes about homework and sometimes not. We would let her lead the conversation. After about ten minutes we would leave, wishing her a good night's work on the way out. And of course we built flexibility into the plan. If her grades ever took a nosedive,

we would take it as a sign that she was inviting us into her homework worries, to which we would respond accordingly. Well, that was two months ago and we haven't had to nag her once in that time. And most important, we still feel like good parents. In fact, my husband and I both genuinely look forward to our family tea time each evening.

A strategy that some parents use to encourage motivation is good, old-fashioned bribery. That is, money (or things) for grades. Bribes seldom work, though, mainly because the teenager doesn't internalize the good feelings that come from working hard; in fact, the material reward typically obfuscates these feelings. The only time I've heard of this bribery approach working was when it was used as a one-time intervention.

We were very frustrated with Sheila's academic performance during her first two years of high school, but then prior to her junior year we did what had been previously unimaginable to us. We bribed her! But we did it with a long-range purpose in mind. Before the beginning of the semester, we sat down and expressed our disappointment at her not doing better in school. We felt that she wasn't turned on to learning, and, worst of all, she was afraid to really push herself 100 percent. It was as if she were afraid of discovering that maybe she wasn't actually all that intelligent; it seemed safer for her to be lazy. Anyway, we came up with a bribe that everyone agreed to (I'm still too embarrassed to admit what it was). The motivation (bribe) was sufficient enough to outweigh her hesitation and fear at giving 100 percent academically. So we set high standards and got out of the way. She knew this was a one-time offer and that we were doing it so she could feel the success that comes from giving her all.

Well, it worked. She got terrific grades and written reports (along with the promised reward) and she broke through her fear. In fact, for the duration of high school she maintained her high academic standards. At one point she even thanked us, saying that in the long run it was much more satisfying, fun, and easier to go all-out than to flake off!

This brings up another important point: the experience of giving 100 percent. With all that is happening in the adolescent world, it is far too easy for teenagers to become afraid of total effort. As parents, you want to encourage your adolescents to find a place where they can give their all—in classes, sports, clubs, music, the arts—regardless of the results. They need to experience how success is less about talent than persistence. Or, as Albert Einstein once said, "Genius is 1 percent inspiration and 99 percent perspiration." This experience of all-out effort becomes an important reference point to them as they grow and mature into adulthood; and with the proper nudging, this experience will transfer to other aspects of the adolescent's life.

> I [author] once talked with a sophomore girl about her poor, and getting worse, academic performance. She was very concerned but didn't seem motivated to change anything. She was quite passive. Fortunately I remembered that she was a terrific basketball player, so I began to ask her about her approach to big games. All of a sudden she became very animated and passionate; not a trace of passivity remained! After a bit I reflected aloud that she sure seemed to play to win. She nodded quite assuredly. And then I added, "So it is kind of odd to see you playing the academic game so passively; it's like you're playing not to lose rather than playing to win." Her face went from assuredness to confusion to conviction in the space of a few seconds. Academics and 100 percent effort were now in a framework that she understood. As you can imagine, the conversation took a dramatic turn after that, and it was without much surprise to both of us that she turned her academic spin around in the ensuing months.

Whatever transpires, the final goal is rather simple when it comes to schoolwork. Realize that if parents worry too much it doesn't leave any worrying available to the adolescent. The goal is to give the appropriate amount of worrying back to the teenager so she can begin to take responsibility. And, it is essential to find a pace of handing over the worries and responsibility that works for everyone. Go too fast and she feels abandoned and overwhelmed. Go too slow and she feels belittled.

Finally, your adolescent's ongoing relationships to grades is a baseline for your understanding of her world. Any sudden and dramatic change in her grades usually reflect other changes in her life. Undue stress and anxiety in other areas often reveal themselves most obviously in grades.

> When my parents were getting divorced (and for about a year afterward), I had the hardest time concentrating on schoolwork. My brain was fuzzy and I couldn't stay focused for more than a few minutes before my mind would just sort of take off. It sucked. I remember hours of staring at the same history paragraph without understanding a bit of it. And it wasn't like I was thinking intensely about anything else. I was just drifting all over the place. It was like my concentration was drunk.

In response to this phenomena, a student and I formulated what we call the "Homework Anti-Worrying Technique." It has been quite useful to a number of students over the years.

Homework Anti-Worrying Technique

1. As you sit down to study, put a pile of blank scraps of paper in the upper-right-hand corner of your desk.

2. Begin studying. Whenever a worry, concern, or vague drifting thought occurs, take a slip of paper and as concisely as possible (in four or five words) write down the worry. Then put the paper, face down, in a pile in the upper-left-hand corner of your desk. Continue studying.

3. Whenever you notice yourself drifting, repeat Step 2 and then resume studying.

4. End your studying time a half hour early. Remove your books and the blank sheets of paper from your desktop.

5. Take the pile that you've written on and browse through the sheets. Pick one and think about it for awhile. When you're done, pick another. Go through the entire pile or think about these concerns for a half hour, whichever comes first.

6. Go do something enjoyable for at least a little while.

This technique is simple and useful to students at times of high stress. Until they learn to put aside their worries internally, it is easier and more efficient to put aside their worries externally.

Finally, use your developing understanding of their world to creatively and gracefully assist them to handle their various pressures. Encourage them to recruit you into their solutions.

> Last year I had terrible grades—so bad, in fact, that I was on the verge of getting expelled. Part of the trouble was that schoolwork seemed to come real easy to my friends, so I was the only one flunking out. Anyway, a big part of the problem was that while my friends were supportive of me and everything, they still didn't take "no" for an answer when I said I had to stay in over the weekend to study. I mean, I started out saying "no," but always ended up going out with them. I guess I just wasn't strong that way. It finally got so bad that one day the vice principal told me that if my grades didn't get much better very soon, then I had better start looking for another school. So that night I finally broke down in front of my mom and told her how scared I was. Well, to make a long story short we decided she would be the "bad mom" from then on, at least with my friends. So that Saturday when they called me to go out I said that my mom wouldn't let me (she was standing right next to me when I said it). Then when my friend started giving me a hard time my mom screamed at me to get off the phone. Then I started screaming back at her and we had a real vicious argument (all fake, of course) while my friend listened on the phone. It was actually a lot of fun! Maybe it wasn't the most honest way in the world, but at least it worked.

CHAPTER 9

Sex and Romance

My daughter has had the same boyfriend for more than a month now. What do I need to know about her sex life? Is there anything I should say or do?

Let's start with the less-anxiety producing topic of romance since, ideally, sex develops out of romantic relationships. First love is an unparalleled phenomenon. Nothing can match it in terms of excitement, energy, and positive feelings. Also, if this significant relationship occurs when your adolescent is in high school, it is all the more exciting for him or her because it seems to resolve other issues of adolescence (see Chapter 2).

Romantic relationships expand adolescents' social lives (they now spend time with their boyfriend's or girlfriend's social group as well as their own) and they have an intimate best friend, which meets their increasing friendship and intimacy demands. This is crucial. Teenagers now have somebody they are open with and who is reciprocally open with them. They are sharing things they've never shared before. Additionally, they are deeply concerned with one another's well-being, which simultaneously feels good and somewhat cracks through their necessarily egocentric world. Trust and compassion are built up through their relationship. Finally there is somebody who they feel truly understands them. On the personal identity side, dramatic changes are happening: "Here is someone I admire, and not only do they spend time with me, but they admire me too. Therefore, I must be an admirable and good person!" Talk about a confidence-builder at the right time.

Take a moment to reflect on your first experience of being in love:

♦ How did it make you feel about yourself to be in love and to be loved?

♦ How did this first love affect problems or concerns in other areas of your life?

♦ How did it affect your relationships with your parents? Your friends?

So, when a teenager experiences that first love, it makes sense that he will organize his life around that person. In the presence of this person, he feels cared for, listened to, desirable, and admired all at a time when this kind of feedback is not readily available (see Chapter 2). It is no wonder that the couple will spend hours talking on the phone, and will see each other whenever possible during the school day.

> I love being in love. It's wonderful! We wait for each other between classes; have lunch together; and generally spend as much time as possible together. It's not that we're always talking, either; sometimes we're pretty quiet—even on the phone. Sometimes, when we talk late at night, we even fall asleep on the phone with each other. It just feels so secure and relaxed to be together. And she feels the same way, which is what's so great.

Of course, most of these first loves are not everlasting, no matter what most teenagers think at the time. However, if you state this directly it will be felt as quite demeaning and will be met with the most venomous of reactions. Remember, this is his first love, not his third or fourth, so he doesn't have a backdrop of experience to draw from. In fact, this first love is so novel and intoxicating in part because it is all uncharted territory.

> Watching my daughter go through the pain and ecstacy of first love has been such an experience for me. I feel like I'm going through it all again, except this time I'm buffered from the pain by experience, but unfortunately I'm also buffered from the joy by experience. It makes me envious and thankful at the same time. I'm envious of first

experiences and all the firsts she still has before her, and thankful to not have to live through all that anxiety again!

When this first love comes to an end, it is a very traumatic event in any adolescent's life, especially if she doesn't want the relationship to end (What was it like when your first romantic relationship came to an end?). For most, the ending of the relationship beckons short-term crisis into her life, and definitely dominates her life for awhile. Fortunately, this is usually not too long or too severe. However, in some cases, the ending of the relationship precipitates a full-blown crisis, which is inevitably tied to some other event in her life—such as death of a loved one, divorce, or real or felt abandonment by parents. In these cases, professional help is often necessary (see Chapter 21 for more on this topic).

> When she broke up with me, it was like my world collapsed. I was so depressed it was scary. Half the time I couldn't even get out of bed to go to school. My friends tried to help, but after awhile they got discouraged by my misery. They just couldn't understand why I couldn't get over it. Neither could I. It isn't like I'm the only one to get dumped by a girlfriend! The weird part was that while I knew that I loved her, I also knew it was more than that. Finally my mom dragged me to a psychologist. It took awhile, but the doctor really helped me understand and get through all that was going on. It was like her breaking up with me triggered something much deeper in me.

In the more typical scenario after the breakup (especially if one wasn't the initiator of the breakup), teenagers experience a fairly thorough reorganization of their worlds. Their social life shifts because they now go back to spending both more time with friends and more time with themselves, which is tricky if they have lost touch with friends because of the intensity of the relationship. Adolescents tend to structure their lives around their romantic interests, often excluding others.

> After he broke up with me, I felt like I had nobody. We had gone out for almost a year, and in that time I had pretty much lost close contact with my friends. And I know that

they [friends] were pretty pissed about that. On top of that, they had changed quite a bit over that year, so not only did I have to get them to forgive me, I also had to get to know them all over again. That was actually the hardest part about breaking up: getting my friends back.

Moreover, a teenager's personal identity, which has become fused with his significant other, undergoes a crisis of sorts. He must rethink who he is. Also, he has to rebuild confidence in himself, on his own.

Carrie was so good for me. She knew just what to say to get me to feel good about myself. I was so confident when I was going out with her. I did better in baseball, in my grades, and in my relationship with my parents. I even took more risks when we were going out. Now I just feel shitty about myself, and I don't know how to get out of it. That's what I miss most, my self-confidence.

Clearly, the teenager who initiates the breakup has an easier time of it, but still it is no bed of roses. Many desperately work at maintaining the friendship even though the romance is gone, but this is no easy task. Some do this out of a genuine desire to maintain the friendship and some to alleviate their guilt; usually it is a combination of both.

All during the time we were going out we promised each other that if we ever broke up we would still stay friends, no matter what. I mean all that time we were definitely each other's best friend. And after we split up, we tried to stay friends but there was no way it could work. I just wanted to be friends, but he still wanted more. So as a result I couldn't tell him about the parts of my life that would hurt him [interests in other guys]. It was really weird and tense all the time between us. Finally we had a big argument, I mean really big. We haven't spoken for over a month now. Hopefully we can be friends sometime down the road, but I'm not sure. I think we tried to be good friends too soon after we broke up. I think we needed some time apart before trying to be friends, but it's too late now.

After the breakup of a serious romance, your teenager needs gentle and quiet support from you and your family. She may not need or want to discuss the relationship, but be assured she needs your quiet understanding.

My parents were real cool about it [her break up with her boyfriend]. They didn't ask me a million questions or anything, but it isn't like they didn't want to. They were there for me, but they weren't pushy. And they did all sorts of nice little things for me: made me my favorite foods, bought me flowers a couple of times, and generally hung around the house more than they usually do. They even looked the other way when I was on the phone after 11:00.

Now to the topic that dominates much of the adolescent landscape: sex. It was confusing enough prior to AIDS, but now it is even more frightening and anxiety-producing. In modern times teenage sex is often, to say the least, problematic: teenagers' bodies are fully capable and desirous of sex, but they are not yet adults by society's standards. Sexual feelings and sexual urges are powerful forces in teenagers' lives. Few are prepared for the complications and disruptions from these emergent sexual drives. For many, it is like their bodies and their minds are on entirely different wavelengths (take a moment to remember your own experience as a teenager.) Sex is also potentially dangerous and often carries with it a variety of moral injunctions. Further complicated by effective but less-than-perfect birth control that makes it possible to have sex without having children—but also possible to still take precautions and get pregnant.

According to a recent cover story in *Time* magazine (May 1993), 19 percent of thirteen- to fifteen-year-olds have had sexual intercourse, and 55 percent of sixteen- to seventeen-year-olds have had sexual intercourse. Remember, adolescents typically turn thirteen in the seventh grade and fifteen in the ninth grade. The *Time* article cites three reasons for these statistics. First, adolescents undergo earlier physical maturation: "The onset of menstruation in girls has dropped three months each decade, so the urges that once landed at fourteen may now hit at twelve." Second, the media blitz: "Teenagers typically watch five hours of television a day—which in a year means they have seen nearly fourteen thousand sexual encounters, according to the Center for Population Options." Worse yet, the majority of these encounters is seen through the idealized lens of the television camera. In the fantasy world of television, most sexual encounters are glamorized and adequately resolved by the end of the hour (or by the end of the minute in commercials). In most cases, sex is elevated above relationships, a subject which receives little attention or education in comparison (see Chapter 11). Also, each of these sexual encounters explicitly communicates a black-and-white image of beauty, with the implicit message that if you fit this description, life is endless bliss. They represent a standard against which to measure oneself, but which no one can ever match. Adolescent girls are most susceptible here (see Chapter 15).

Third, and I believe most important, sex is a short-term means of bolstering low self-esteem: "Kids can't say no if they don't first learn how to feel good about themselves," former Surgeon General Joycelyn Elders states in the *Time* article. With the excitement of the sexual encounter comes the message that you are attractive, valued, and desired by another—a powerful, irresistible message to most teenagers who don't feel good about themselves on a daily basis. From this perspective, sex is an oasis of self-esteem for both males and females.

> It's exciting to really like somebody. And part of the fun is getting them to like you back. It's a real turn-on. And the physical part is a real trip. The fact that this person not only lets you touch them but enjoys it is totally cool. In fact, once the physical stuff heats up it can take awhile to figure out if you really even like this person or not. It all gets tied together—sometimes in a big old knot!

In an ideal world, the road to sex is paved with lots of information and conversation about its mechanical and emotional aspects. Parents play important roles in many of these conversations. If you are too shy or embarrassed to talk about it yourself, you still need to make sure these conversations are taking place. Don't let your personal discomfort cost you your adolescent's life, and don't assume the schools are handling these issues. "The standard curriculum now consists of one or two days in fifth grade dealing with puberty; two weeks in an eighth grade health class dealing with anatomy, reproduction, and AIDS prevention, and perhaps a twelfth grade elective course on current issues in sexuality," according to the *Time* article.

Face it, most schools don't do better with this subject than most parents. And given the number of teenagers engaged in sex, this is a major gap in adolescents' education. So, what is a parent to do? Talk with your kids; hopefully the awkwardness will go away, but then again it may not.

> The first time I talked with my daughter about sex and AIDS we were very uncomfortable. And while it did get better over time, it didn't get a whole lot better. Now she's a senior in college and we laugh about those conversations, but not without acknowledging their importance.

Awkward or not, these conversations *must* take place. You also have to provide other avenues for these conversations, perhaps through older siblings, a friend that is comfortable with the topic and friendly with your teenager, or a prearranged series of visits to Planned Parenthood. The options are limited only by your creativity—just don't let your creativity be paralyzed by your anxiety.

> After I watched a TV special on AIDS, I was scared and guilty because I've never talked with Sid [son] about any of this. I'm just too embarrassed. So I called his physician the next day and asked if he would talk to Sid at his next checkup. He chuckled a bit and said that it wouldn't be the first time he had responded to such a request. So we set up a routine physical for Sid later that month. I feel much better knowing that he has had the conversation at least once.

When evaluating your adolescent's sex life, don't assume anything and don't rule anything out either. The bottom line is that you have little control over what she actually does or doesn't do, but you do have a certain amount of influence, especially in the areas of health and safety.

You can at least have a conversation with her on the topic (without asking directly what she is or isn't doing, which would be too intrusive for any adolescent to tolerate gracefully). Express your values as well as your pragmatic concerns. Speaking in the "what if" realm, you can let her know that while you don't approve of sexual intercourse at this age (if you don't), you are much more concerned about her overall well-being. Thus, talk about birth control options and how to go about obtaining them, go to Planned Parenthood, make an appointment with a physician, have your daughter see a gynecologist, and so on.

> I'm not sure that it is the right thing to do, but I bought a box of condoms and put them in my son's room. And I told him that if he ever wants more just to leave me a note. While I don't approve of teenage sex, I'm not naive either. And my attitude definitely isn't worth my son's life!

Be graceful about this topic, without necessarily approving. Also, don't assume your adolescent is one of the 55 percent, for he may be greatly offended if you make this assumption and it doesn't apply. (Remember, 45 percent of sixteen- and seventeen-year-olds have *not* had sex.) Or, as Dr. Ruth Westheimer exhorts: "teach kids everything, and then encourage them to wait."

> Since her father died several years ago, my daughter [a senior] and I have been very close. We even talk about sex sometimes. Recently she said, without my prompting, that she and her boyfriend [of ten months] wanted to have sex but were waiting for the right time and place. (She knows I don't approve of sex at her age.) They wanted a time when they could be comfortable and a place where they could snuggle and hold each other afterwards. They both want their first time to be special, and therefore are willing to wait for the right circumstances.

A few closing words on this topic. The topic of sex demands communication from the parent-adolescent relationship in four essential ways. First, it is not a value-free topic, nor should it ever be. Teenagers need to know where you stand on this subject. The most obvious reason for this is that they need a clear opinion (structure) to ground them and guide them in their internal decision-making process. Second, adolescents need to have significant information which *is* value-free on basic anatomy, birth control, safe sex, and sexually transmitted diseases. Along with this are discussions about relationships and their emotional and interpersonal ramifications, all of which need to be addressed in a variety of settings over time. Third, parents have little direct control over what happens. The best you can do is make sure your teenager has the information, knows your values on the subject, and is experienced in learning from consequences. Finally, no matter what happens, you need to make sure that your love for your adolescent is communicated above and beyond everyone's anxiety and judgment about sexual relations and behavior.

CHAPTER 10

Being Gay

My son is in his junior year and I'm worried because he seems to have no interest in girls. Could he be gay? And if he is, what can I do?

To begin with, there is no stereotypical manner in which gay people act. An effeminate manner in males and a masculine manner in women are by no means signs of homosexuality. Nor is an apparent lack of interest in the opposite sex necessarily a sign of homosexuality. With everything else that is happening in the typical adolescent's life, don't be surprised if some don't pursue an active interest in the opposite sex until after high school (somewhat analogous to this situation are the teenagers who aren't interested in obtaining their driver's license, which doesn't mean they aren't interested in obtaining their independence). There are other reasons besides sexual orientation that may account for this apparent lack of active interest in the opposite sex. (See Chapter 2 for more on this.)

But for now, let's suppose that your teenager is gay. Given that between 5 percent and 10 percent[1] of the population is gay, then it is probable that an equal if not greater percentage of parents have gay teenagers (since many parents have more than one child). Also, if adolescents are aware of their homosexuality, it is probably the single most powerful organizing factor in their life and dominates all other horizons described in Chapter 2.

There is no one common experience of the gay adolescent, but there are some common themes and questions that need resolving. After we address these, we'll move to the question of the parent's role.

The first step in acknowledging homosexuality is to recognize it in oneself. This is different for everybody. While some may know as early as middle school, others won't fully recognize their sexuality until sometime in adulthood. But for now, we'll limit this conversation to adolescents who are aware of their sexuality. Initially teenagers may attempt to hide their sexuality from themselves, or even to change their sexuality. Many gay adolescents date the opposite sex and have hetero-sexual relationships to try to disprove their gayness. They are literally acting on the thesis: "If I am sexual with the opposite sex it will prove that I'm not gay."

> Initially I was frantic not to be a lesbian. Not only did I date lots of guys, but I was also quite promiscuous with them. Somehow I felt like this erased all the strong feelings I was having for women. Needless to say, it didn't work, but it sure fooled everybody around me. People just couldn't believe it when I finally came out.

Again, as with much of adolescent behavior, the signals sent through their sexual behaviors are mixed and complex. Try not to forget this or jump to conclusions.

Actually, according to sexuality researcher Dr. Alfred Kinsey, there are varying degrees of homosexual aspects in most of us. That is, gay and straight are not discreet categories; rather, they represent the ends of a sexuality continuum. Combine this with all the other adolescent changes, and it's no wonder that sexual confusion is sometimes a neces-sary phase in determining sexual identity.

Recognizing gay aspects in oneself and fully acknowledging it to oneself are two very different things. But by the time teenagers acknowledge their gayness, they are usually quite certain of it; if there has been any hesitancy it has been dispelled by the strength and persis-tence of their gay feelings. But acknowledging gayness is not the biggest or most difficult step; accepting it is. Given that being gay still carries a strong social stigma in society, it is not something that most adolescents welcome with open arms. Typically they try to fight it as much as possible, in part because of the lack of social acceptance and in part because it may not fit with the long-term image they have of themselves. Many children nurture the dream of growing up and getting a good job, getting married, and raising a family. Few nurture the dream of growing up gay, discovering prejudice in the workplace, fighting the legal system to have your intimate relationship recognized as legitimate, and overqualifying yourself in order to adopt children. In addition, before they can accept their own gayness, teenagers must first undo the stereotypes about homosexuals that they have grown up with. Homophobia is not limited to heterosexuals.

> Realizing I was gay was no big deal. I mean, how could I avoid it with the way I felt around attractive men? The difficult part was accepting my homosexuality. I grew up with all sorts of ideas about the kinds of people who were gay: men who dressed in women's clothing, men who molested little boys, men who were promiscuous, and men who were very effeminate. None of these stereotypes fit me, but still I knew that I was gay. I was captain of my football team and wanted desperately to fall in love with a guy my age and have a steady relationship. None of the stereotypes I grew up with fit.

Probably the single greatest fear adolescent gays have is rejection by their family and friends, especially family. It is this deep-seated fear that I believe places these teenagers in the highest risk category of their peers. Imagine, if you can, what it would be like to know something about yourself that you believe could lead to total rejection from your family if they found out—a fact so horrible that they would expel you from the family. This is the reality for many gay teenagers. They develop this attitude from personal and societal stereotypes of homosexuality as well as from explicit and implicit views about gayness in their home.

> I've known that I'm homosexual for several years now, but I still haven't come out to my family. I'm pretty sure that my mom could handle it, but I doubt that my dad could. And I know that my mom could never keep it from my dad. He's just this sort of macho guy who loves sports and acting like

a man's man. On top of that he is always making gay jokes, which makes me sure he'd freak. I'll probably wait until I'm in college. I think the distance and time apart will make it more bearable. Also, hopefully I'll meet others who have already come out to their families.

A teenager's secret about being gay can eat away at his developing personal identity and general self-esteem. He believes that sure, he may be successful in many activities, but still, if his sexuality were found out and the truth was known, all his achievements would be wiped out in one fell swoop. Also, many gay adolescents often begin to believe that somehow they deserve this fate—that underneath it all they must actually be bad people. Unchecked, this can lead to strong feelings of self-loathing and even self-destructive behaviors.

For the longest time, I felt that somehow I deserved my homosexuality, that underneath I was a terrible person. During the worst of it I took some outrageous chances. I felt like if I survived them then maybe I deserved to live after all. I used to get stoned and drive the car really fast; I would get drunk and walk along high ledges in dangerous places; and once I even played Russian roulette with myself—putting one bullet in my dad's gun and pulling the trigger; fortunately once was enough to feel like I didn't deserve to die.

Avoidance or refusal to accept gayness can eventually destroy an adolescent. According to a 1986 study conducted by Paul Gibson for the U.S. Department of Health & Human Services, gay and lesbian youths are two to three times more likely to attempt suicide than heterosexual youths, and up to 30 percent of successful teen suicides may have to do with sexual identity issues. These startling statistics don't even take into account other risk-taking behaviors motivated by sexual identity problems, such as drug and alcohol abuse.

Before I began to accept my homosexuality, I was pretty crazy. I got stoned and drunk all the time. In fact, I managed to become an alcoholic. It was in A.A. that it became clear that I had to address my sexuality. When I was drinking I would engage in unsafe homosexual sex and then blame it all on the alcohol; that way I never had to believe I was gay. In retrospect I can see that it was the denial of my sexuality that led to the exaggerated use of alcohol, but nonetheless I managed to become an alcoholic. And ironically, the only way I could get on the wagon was to deal with my sexuality.

Besides family acceptance (addressed later in this chapter), the adolescent needs a group of peers who understand and appreciate the issues faced by gay and lesbian teenagers. They often need access to a supportive community for their developing sense of identity: other gay teenagers. Thankfully, these types of networks are becoming more frequent these days, but they are still not readily accessible to most adolescents.

The really hard part was finding other gays and lesbians at school to talk with. Because of the stigma attached to homosexuality by peers, family, and society, it isn't easy to find each other. It's kind of crazy. For a long time I traveled across town to a support group for gay teenagers, which was very helpful at first. I got to hear other people's stories, fears, successes, and failures. Suddenly I didn't feel quite so alone. And they were very helpful in my coming-out process to my parents, giving me lots of advice and general encouragement. But after awhile I realized that with most of them the only thing I had in common was my sexuality. They were interested in very different things than I was and attended different schools all over town. All of a sudden I felt the split of living in two worlds simultaneously and yet never in one completely. My sexuality was set apart from my daily life at school. So I began selectively coming out to friends at school. It was with mixed results, but by the time I graduated most of my close friends knew. Anyway, it wasn't until college that my two worlds came together. There is a strong Gay and Lesbian Alliance at my college and it helps a lot.

Gay peer groups are important because they represent a place where adolescents' sexuality is accepted as a normal part of them, not some secret to keep hidden. And remember how important acceptance is during the teenage years.

When adolescents do come to a conscious realization and acceptance of their gayness, they must make some decisions: Are they going to come out to anybody? If so, who? How and when? Can any family members handle their coming out? Can they deal with others who don't accept their sexuality? Is it worth the risk? Are they going to be active sexually or are they going to put it on hold until after high school or some later date? If they are going to be active, where is a safe place? Could they handle their classmates learning about their being gay? Do they feel an obligation to speak out? Are there others who feel like they do? How can they find one another? Are there any "safe" adults with whom to talk?

So, what do you do if your teenager is gay and comes out to you?[2] Once you learn of your adolescent's sexuality, you can expect your world to shift quite dramatically. Parents are seldom prepared for a child's homosexuality, and as a result have quite a bit of catching up to do. First, when your teenager comes out, don't doubt her. By the time she is telling you, she is quite sure of her sexuality. As mentioned earlier, her main fear is rejection from the family, so you can be sure that she won't risk this rejection unless she is certain. Second, she cannot change; you are the one that must do the changing.

> It was really quite a trip; it was like they [parents] were reading from a script or something. Initially they were speechless, but once their voices came back their first question was, "Are you sure?" I mean by the time I could even think of telling them I had to be absolutely sure myself. How could they think I would tell them something like this unless I was sure! After a long while they finally got that I was quite sure of my sexuality. Then, following this "Parent of a Gay Teenager" script, they took another approach, wondering if it might just be a phase I was going through. At

which point my mom cited a friend who thought he was gay until he met the "right" woman! Dad took it even further, wondering aloud if possibly I couldn't change. It was crazy!

And,

I must admit that when Sarah came out to me, it took me by complete surprise. And I'm afraid I didn't react very well. I was angry and confused. I felt like she was doing this to me. I was so self-absorbed that I couldn't imagine what she was telling me from any perspective other than my own. I was worried about what my family and friends would think, as well as how I would tell them. It was all so confusing to me. And not just her sexuality. Probably the most difficult part was in letting go of all the dreams I had for her: getting married to a man we liked, having children, and most of all, becoming a grandmother. While we worked to understand and accept the implications of what Sarah was telling us, it was by no means either smooth or easy. In retrospect, I can see that it was us who had to change and begrudgingly get caught up to our daughter. Thank goodness she was both insistent and patient with us; we had a great deal of growing up to do.

What your gay teenager needs more than anything else is your acceptance and love of him and an honest reaction. You can be confused, angry, or frightened, and still assure him of your continuing love and acceptance. He doesn't expect you to immediately accept what it has taken him so long to accept. But he does expect and need you to work with him toward honest acceptance. And considering how important parental and family acceptance is, he will usually be quite patient and open with you during this process. Also, genuine acceptance paves the way for new hopes and new joys in your relationship with your teenager.

Finally, for yourself, don't try to do it alone. Make use of organizations like P-Flag (Parents and Friends of Lesbians and Gays[3]) for education and support. Hearing other parents' stories, struggles, and victories is a great source of support and inspiration. (This approach goes for many parenting issues: alcohol, drugs, eating disorders, depression, or just general parenting concerns.)

Endnotes

1. No two groups or studies are able to agree on the exact percentage of gays in this country. From the work of Alfred Kinsey (1948 and 1953) emerged a figure of 10 percent. But in a recent study by researchers at the University of Chicago (Laumann and others, 1993), 5.3 percent of men and 3.5 percent of women acknowledged having sex with a same-sex partner at least once since puberty. In this same study, 2.8 percent of men and 1.4 percent of women identified themselves as homosexual or bisexual. Personally, I don't believe the exact percentages are critical to know. What is critical is that homosexuality is a fact of life in our society. Even if the percentage were only 1 percent, that would still be a lot of people.

2. Some adolescents who are unable to come out to you directly will do so in a variety of indirect manners, such as leaving gay literature in your sight. But don't jump to any conclusions, and also don't keep yourself unnecessarily naive.

3. P-Flag, P.O. Box 20308, Denver, Colorado, 80220

❧ CHAPTER 11 ❦

Television, Music, and Computers

*What about all the music teenagers
listen to and the television they watch?
Should I monitor any of this?*

To many parents, music and TV seem like variations of the same subject, but they are quite different.

A couple of years ago I read an interview of the highest-ranking student at the University of California in Berkeley. He said, quite simply, that he believed the greatest influence on his G.P.A. was growing up without a television in the house!

One aspect of television that, I believe, is harmful to adolescents' psychological development is the contrived and simplified emotional aspects of the shows and characters. Even in the most poorly written and badly acted shows, a director can, through the use of camera angles, clichéd lines, and music, manipulate the emotions of an unsuspecting viewer. The illusion created says that I (the viewer) can articulate my emotions; after all, I'm fully capable of experiencing and handling a full range of emotions when I watch TV. Not only is this false but it is also poor modeling for what an articulate emotional life is all about. Only a few shows over the years have attempted a realistic emotional landscape, and they inevitably fade after a few low-rated but artistically recognized seasons. And this is not to say that this is a plot by TV producers; rather, it illustrates the limits of current television.

These limits became clearer to me recently while I was reading Robert Pirsig's latest book, *Lila.* He describes an interchange between himself and Robert Redford over the movie rights to his previous book, *Zen and the Art of Motorcycle Maintenance.* Redford wants the movie rights and wants to make it clear to Pirsig that, as the author, Pirsig is going to be very unhappy with the results, no matter how much he trusts Redford and no matter how much justice Redford attempts to bring to the movie. As I thought about this I recalled professor and author Jerome Bruner's words about plot. A novel has two simultaneous plots: the plot of action (what the characters do), and the plot of consciousness (what the characters are thinking and feeling), which only readers are privy to. This is the basic problem with television and emotional articulation: TV's focus is inevitably on the plot of action and only superficially on the plot of consciousness. We listen to the dialogue between characters and can only extrapolate the consciousness behind it. Real-life emotional processing takes place in the plot of consciousness. Since television is ill-equipped to work with this process, in most television drama, plot of action is exaggerated and simplified to create emotional experiences.

Remember that a teenager's worldview is inherently ambiguous. She needs to learn to function and thrive within this anxious ambiguity, to create clarity within herself. So, when plots of action are presented so clearly on TV it also enhances the ambiguity of her day-to-day life and strengthens her voice of self-criticism. As an example think of a book that you read, enjoyed, and that was later made into a movie. How much shallower were the characters in the movie compared to the book? How was the meaning of the book altered to fit into the dominant plot of action necessary for the screen?

Children, adolescents, and adults need to reflect more on consciousness and less on action if they are to become emotionally mature adults. To the extent that television circumvents this learning process, it is detrimental to one's growth—especially during adolescence.

Now back to the question at hand. I think it makes sense for parents to model the TV-watching behavior they want their kids to exhibit. It also makes sense to make the TV more than the flick of a switch away, for everybody. As for direct monitoring—whether around

TV or numerous other areas—this depends on the age of your teenager. As they get older they need more say in the direction of their lives. So in the most general terms some monitoring is appropriate in ninth grade; less in tenth grade; very little, if any, in eleventh grade; and none in twelfth grade.

> Paul was watching TV nonstop: after school, through dinner, and while he was on the phone with his friends. It was terrible. Finally we had had enough. First we warned him that he could watch all the TV he wanted if his grades didn't go down, but that if his grades went down we would take it as a sign that we needed to step in to assist him in breaking his TV habit. In typical form, he showed no reaction and nothing changed. Then his grades came. We quickly reminded him of the earlier conversation and pulled the plug on the TV, for all of us! The first few weeks were hell. He wouldn't even talk to us. But slowly, things got better. Then the next set of grades came out; not surprisingly, he did much better. So now we negotiate TV-watching and limit it to specific events, for all of us, which is a big change for our family. But anything less would have seemed hypocritical from his viewpoint.

In my more conservative moments, I believe television is a manageable and satisfactory means of entertainment. In more radical moments, well, let's just say I'm not a big advocate. I remember buying my television and expressing my concerns to a friend about the "couch potato" potential in me. He gave me two pieces of advice: one, buy a portable that you keep in a closet when not in use, preferably in a hard-to-reach spot, and two, make sure it doesn't come with a remote control. Make it a pain to get up and change the channel. Most of us need these kinds of external checks.

Music, however, is a different matter (see Chapter 2, in particular Nick's article). Music is an escape that most teenagers use to reflect on the day's activities with muted anxiety. The positive feelings associated with the music give them needed distance and perspective. So believe it or not, they are usually being productive when the headphones are in place and they are sitting on their bed!

> The first thing I do after school is put on my headphones with a favorite CD. At first I just sort of space out, but after awhile I start to think back on the day and all that happened. Somehow it's easier to sort those kinds of things out with music.

A very useful aspect of music is how it helps adolescents articulate what they are feeling. At times, the lyrics actually help them make sense of their feelings. (To fully appreciate this aspect of music, think back to a couple of your favorite and "deepest" songs from adolescence. How profound are the lyrics to your ears now?) Recently a student came into my office with a cassette player and cassette in hand. (A few months ago he had been struggling to articulate how he was feeling about his parents.) As he came in and set up the cassette player, he excitedly said that the song he was about to play summed up precisely how he was feeling. Further, that it was important to hear the music with the words—the words alone didn't capture the full meaning. After the song he told me that understanding exactly what was bothering him had allowed him to figure out what to do. He was quite proud of himself, as he should have been.

Of course, the danger is that the music, like TV, also runs the risk of simplifying a necessarily complex issue in an attempt to take the shortcut. But even in this case, adolescents eventually must come back to the issue when the shortcut doesn't work out.

Finally, there is the question of content (which is a concern similarly shared about certain computer and video games). Historically, it seems that whatever teenagers are into is at least one step beyond their parents' comfort level—remember your parent's response to the music you listened to as a teenager. Remember also how you felt about that response. As in other areas, consider their stage of development—ninth, tenth, eleventh, or twelfth grade—and their ability to compromise. Of course, it is your house and you have the right to insist on certain things; but remember, pick your battles.

Q: What about using computers for games and communication? Where should I draw the line?

There are two aspects to consider: computer and video games and computer communications. Games are a wonderful source of enjoyment for many teenagers. But you should worry when they are playing these games to the exclusion of just about everything else. If your teenager has friends and other interests, then computer games can be quite healthy. But if he comes home after school and does nothing other than play solitary games on his computer, you need to wonder about a lack of social life and a group of friends (see Chapters 2 and 13 for more on these topics). However, this does not mean that solitary computer games and a group of friends are mutually exclusive.

> After school we [three friends] pretty much pick a house and go there until dinner. It may sound odd, but all we do is play computer games. We're really into computers and we all have computers with a bunch of different games on them. Which games we want to play determines which house we go to. All we do is take turns playing games and watching each other. We really don't talk all that much. I know it sounds weird, but it's much better than playing alone.

On the other hand, there is the growing world of computer communications via electronic mail, the Internet, and other computer groups, which are quite fascinating. For adolescents, these modes of communication open new worlds of interpersonal possibilities and intimacy. Now they are no longer limited to conversation with just the other teenagers around them. Potentially they can communicate with anybody else in the world who has a computer and a modem. And probably the most notable aspect of this communication is its expression of pure ideas: the complications of appearance, age, sex, ethnicity, and self-consciousness practically disappear with electronic conversations. In many ways, this method has the advantage of the telephone taken to the extreme. The Internet, for example, is a safe arena in which to develop and experiment with new interpersonal skills. It also forces users to articulate their thoughts through the written word, which is good for teenagers.

> For the most part I talk to people on three different levels. The first is a pretty casual level that I do with all my friends and acquaintances at school. The second is the much deeper level of my true thoughts and feelings. Usually these are pretty confusing at first, so I need some time to figure them out. This is how I use my friends on the Net (The Internet). I got into the Net last year when my boyfriend graduated and went to college a thousand miles away. We both have computers, so it was pretty easy. It's been great for us, but also I've met all sorts of new friends on the Net I don't even know what most of them look like, but still I feel like I know them well. It's safer to talk with them about this kind of stuff. It's easier too. I can say whatever I want and don't have to worry about going out with them the next night or running into them at school. I'm never embarrassed on the Net Not only that, I really tell people what I think of what they say, not like at school where I hold back because I'm afraid of hurting somebody. That's another good thing about the Net: I get honest feedback from people. I don't always like it, but at least it's honest. The third level of communication is what happens with my best friend and my boyfriend. This is basically the same as I communicate on the Net, only it is in person. The Net is an important link between levels of communication for me.

Of course, too much of a good thing is another matter. As with the television, if adolescents can't monitor themselves they may need your assistance; just make sure they are forewarned in time to change the habit on their own if they wish. But clearly, television, music, and computers offer qualitatively different experiences and serve different purposes for teenagers.

CHAPTER 12

Sports and Extracurricular Activities

What role do sports and extracurricular activities play in kids' lives?

Adolescents invest themselves in sports, drama productions, dance, creative arts, and music for essentially the same reasons, though with some important differences.[1] First, playing on a sports team or participating in a production gives teenagers a sense of belonging to a community that has more in common and is generally closer than the greater community of high school. As we saw in Chapter 2, specifically in the social horizon section, belonging helps the teenager deal with self-consciousness and loneliness.

> I enjoy running quite a bit, especially the sense of accomplishment after finishing a good run. Also, it's a great way to snap out of a bad mood. But honestly I enjoy the hanging out before and after practice as much as the actual running. Over the course of a season I come to feel comfortable around these people; I feel more myself at cross-country practice than at any other time during the school day. Plus, as I get to know my teammates I have more people to spend time with during school besides my few close friends. And this lasts beyond the cross-country season. It adds variety to my life.

Second, sports and most extracurricular activities present very clear and concrete challenges. At a time of life when things are less black-and-white and more gray than ever, it is relieving to have these clear challenges. For instance, at the end of a game it is clear which team has won and which has lost. Or at the end of a concert, the audience has either responded to the music or they have not. Also, your performance generally speaks for itself: you play well and you play a lot; you play poorly and you play a little. Of course there are exceptions to every rule: Sometimes a coach or director doesn't recognize an adolescent's talents, and they learn some difficult but essential lessons about life.

> I can't believe I didn't get a part in the play. I had a great audition. And it wasn't just me; everyone there said I was terrific. I mean I thought I was going to get the lead. Instead I got nothing! I'm so pissed! And when I talked to the director, all he could say was that he didn't see it that way. What an ass!

Finally, at least in sports, each day is new and the outcome is unpredictable.

> I enjoy playing soccer every day, whether it is practice or a game, although games are better. Each game tells us if we are getting better and also keeps us humble. (The other day we played a team we had beaten 7 to 1 earlier in the season, and they beat us 3 to 2! We were in a daze the entire game.) But when we are all playing well we are much better than eleven individuals. It's totally cool!

Third, extracurricular activities and athletics present daily opportunities to expand self-confidence. (Remember the discussion in Chapter 2 about declining self-esteem in adolescents, and girls in particular.) Through daily drills, rehearsals, and intra-squad scrimmages, participants have a means of assessing themselves and their improvements. They also have an adult who is often quite invested in their improvement, which, given their more typical perspective of adults, is a refreshing change for most teenagers. In fact, it is often through the coach or director-type relationships that teenagers begin to see adults as other than simply authority figures.

> Coach Johnson is a nut about free-throw shooting. Each of us has to take a hundred shots a day and record the results. But it is kind of cool, too. I mean over time I get to see how much I've improved. And even when he yells I know it's because he wants me to get better and that he has my best interests as a player and our best interests as a team in mind. Also, with all of us doing it together it becomes kind of a bonding thing for the team. So, I guess it makes sense, even though I still don't really like it.

Fourth, athletics and extracurricular activities help organize adolescents' lives. Most teams and productions practice a few hours each day during the season, which leaves less available time for other teenage activities: schoolwork, family responsibilities, and maintaining a social life. As a result, most teenagers must become much better organized during the season (when they have less time) than out of the season (when they have more time). With the production or sport as a priority, they organize themselves around it. (It is no surprise that most student-athletes do better academically in season than out of season.) Adolescents do well with lots of activities, provided that most of what they do is structured through consistent practice times and game and production schedules. This is why musicians practice better when performing with a group or taking regularly scheduled lessons. The lesson or group organizes them and their practice.

A common error adults make about teenagers is that they try to understand what is best for their teenager through a strictly rational framework. For instance, if students are slipping in their grades, it is not uncommon for parents to insist that they drop their involvement in, say, the basketball team. But, given the loss of this organizing factor in their lives (not to mention their loss of autonomy), their grades slip even further. The parent's intervention works in the opposite direction that logic would indicate is correct. Does this mean that parents should always intervene in the least logical manner? No. It does mean that you must talk with and listen to your teenager to understand what the slipping grades mean and what participation on the team means.

> Sophia was doing poorly in school when she came home and told us that she made lead in the spring play at school. Obviously we were quite happy for her, yet we were disturbed at how we imagined this would affect her grades. When we brought this up she broke into tears and became very fearful that we would insist that she drop the play (which we had planned to suggest!). We listened as she explained how important the play was to her. She promised that if we would support her in this, she would do better in school. In fact, she suggested that we call her teachers after the first month of rehearsals to make sure that she was improving. Since she had never shown this kind of initiative or responsibility before, we grudgingly went along with her proposal. Well, she stayed involved in the play, did wonderfully in her role, and even improved her grades. It was quite an eye-opener for us.

Finally, these long-term commitments to activities (especially to a group of people) are important in teaching adolescents how to get through their egocentricity and personal doubt in order to accomplish something of their choosing. Much of what it takes to become successful in life depends on how one handles doubt and adversity while working to achieve a goal. If doubt and adversity get the better of people, then they seldom accomplish their goals and even more seldomly delve into anything in-depth. Extracurricular activities are literally ongoing workshops in addressing doubt and challenge, and the lessons learned here transfer to the classroom and to life.

A major difference between good students and poor students lies in how they view a difficult problem on a test. Poor students see the problem and panic, often talking to themselves in a manner that supports doubt: "I knew I didn't study enough for this test. I can't believe I don't know this; I don't even know where to start! I'm sure the rest are even more difficult. I'm going to flunk for sure. Look at everyone else, they're just cruising right along. I'm so stupid I can't believe it!" Good students, however, see the problem, and with self-confidence, begin to dissect it: "This is difficult, but if I stay with it long enough I know I can figure out where to begin. And from there, all I have to do is stay calm and patient and it'll begin to come together, just like a puzzle. Ahh, there is something I know. Not much, but at least a beginning." This same thought process is experienced and lived through in extra-curricular activities. Obviously the more committed one is to the activity, the more directly these issues are confronted.

Obviously, there is a great deal happening when your teenager gets involved with an extracurricular program or a sport—at least as much as has been discussed so far, and probably much more. Your best bet is to support these activities even though you may not fully understand them. Also, especially if your teenager is particularly talented at one activity or another, be careful not to make that activity the core of their identity. Your esteem, and theirs' too, is much safer when it's focused on supporting them as a full person, rather than when it's dependent on them succeeding at some event or achieving some specific goal.

Endnote

1. The following discussion, while most directly about sports, is also true for drama, student government, creative arts, music, and similar activities.

CHAPTER 13

Making Friends

My son is having trouble making friends.
I know there is not much that I can do,
but should I be advising him somehow?

Given that loneliness (see Chapter 2) is one of the most powerful and painful forces in teenagers' lives, watching your teenager struggle to make friends can be heart-wrenching. Unfortunately, parents cannot do much directly. There is very little useful advice you can offer that he will take advantage of, which is not to say that you do not have useful suggestions. Even when he seeks your advice, he'll often resist what you have to offer. In fact, he may resent you for offering what he asked for! Here's why.

When adolescents ask for your advice (on just about anything) they are often asking for something else. Basically they seek your advice because they have momentarily lost belief in themselves, and what they are seeking is not your advice so much as your belief in them. They want to borrow your belief in them until they can restore their own belief in themselves.

> For a long time whenever Miles asked my advice I assumed he wanted suggestions. Given the long silences between us I was more than ready to be helpful, so I gave lots of suggestions. But he inevitably got sharp with me and never followed any of my suggestions. In fact, things usually got worse and he got more passive. But finally one day it clicked. When he offered the bait by asking my advice I side-stepped

the trap with a different response: "Wow, that's a tough one. What do you think? I mean, what have you tried so far? Well, I'm not really sure, but I know you'll figure it out; you seem to manage pretty well. If you come up with anything else or want me as a sounding board let me know." And the less advice I offer the more he talks to me!

This simultaneous seeking and refusing behavior has to do with the development of a personal identity during adolescence, which includes moving away from (but not becoming disconnected from) family and establishing independence. Suppose you try to help? On the one hand, he welcomes your efforts (after all, he's asking for your assistance), but on the other hand, he resents you for your intervention, as it only spotlights his dependence on you (this moving away process is about independence and showing that he doesn't need you as much anymore). Since he is in this dilemma, you can expect inconsistency.

As a kid I was a fanatical basketball player. I played in all sorts of leagues and practiced daily at the hoop behind my house. My father also happened to be a basketball coach—a very successful one. This was both a blessing and a curse. I can still painfully remember many nights during the ninth and tenth grades when I would cajole him into coming outside to watch some new move or to get some feedback on my jumpshot. After a bit he would succumb to my requests and join me out back. From then on the pattern was fairly standard. He would watch closely while rebounding the ball for me; would compliment me on a couple of areas; and would point out one or two things I could do to improve. For the first ten minutes I enthusiastically worked on his suggestions, often implementing them with great success. But after a few more minutes I found myself getting mysteriously resentful. In fact, while implementing his suggestions I found myself trying to disprove their validity through self-sabotage! When he inevitably corrected me I stiffened. Well, as you can imagine, from there it was a short step into an argument, with one of us (usually me) storming off the court and into the house and both of us making sure to let my mother know that the other one was indeed crazy! But no matter how predictable this pattern was, we each clung to it stubbornly.

Now, back to the issue of friends. Without friends, moving toward independence is quite difficult, and given the influence of loneliness (especially at this age), lacking friends can become quite an impediment to healthy development (see Chapter 7).

In assessing the problem, ask yourself, "Does my teenager have friend-making abilities? Did he have friends in middle and elementary schools?" If the answer is yes, then with time he will probably find a niche of friends, and most likely all he needs is some support and borrowed belief in himself. With a history of friend-making abilities behind him, one could view what is happening now as a temporary aberration. What can you do about this, then? What follows is a sample letter of what I might send to a student experiencing such an aberration.

Dear Jim,

When we met earlier this week you expressed concerns over your recent inability to make friends in high school. This has surprised you, given the ease with which you made friends in middle school and continue to make friends in various sports camps during summers. After a bit of discussion we agreed that the problem seems more situational than personal, but if it doesn't change in the near future it has the potential to become personal, something you very much want to avoid.

After further discussion you realized there wasn't much more you could do to secure friends without being untrue to yourself—an approach that neither of us advocates. So we were momentarily stuck, until we came up with the "What the hell!" solution. Once this was on the table you exploded with ideas—well, after you overcame some initial doubts and hesitations. It was time to experiment; we brainstormed all the things that you could experiment with at school in order to break up your current non-friendship patterns and simultaneously follow up on some interests while pushing yourself to learn more about your school. Your ideas included: go to a swim meet, attend a Student Council meeting as a visitor, work with the technical crew on the winter play, get involved with the homecoming celebration, find out about the various clubs at school and attend one or two of the meetings that seemed interesting, go on an outdoor education trip, volunteer to tutor one day a week at your old middle school, write an article for the paper, check out the peer counseling office, and so on. Your list was much longer than this; these are just a few of the ideas I remembered.

From there you committed to following through on two ideas in the next week. And I must say, Jim: When you left my office you seemed quite relieved and excited about your new direction. I'm curious as to how it goes. Keep me updated.

The lack of friends is more worrisome when teenagers don't have experiences of friendship and making friends somewhere in their history. The same process described with Susan can work, but it takes more persistence and presence on the part of the adults involved. Probably the most important thing you can do is be on the look out for "red flags," signs that loneliness is getting the better of adolescents and involving them in at-risk activities: using alcohol or drugs, skipping school, and sleeping all day. These are clear invitations for professional help (see Chapter 21 for more on this subject).

So, what can you do to help your teenager through all this? I advocate an indirect approach (which is often very successful in many other areas). First, see if you can get other adults (not your spouse) involved in the situation—ideally a school counselor, teacher, or coach. Talk to them about the problem, but not with the expectation that they will do anything about it other than be aware. If they have a good relationship with your adolescent, perhaps they will feel comfortable bringing up the topic in a future conversation. Chances are that your teenager will more readily take advice from someone other than either you or your spouse, mainly because the relationship is one of the adolescent's choosing. (Non-parent adults who teenagers have chosen to have a relationship with are important resources for both adolescents and parents.)

Also, feel free to communicate on this topic with your teenager through notes or letters. This circumvents a number of potential problems. First, it allows him to save face, and removes him from the independence/dependence power struggle. Second, because this struggle is minimized, it allows him to "hear" what you are saying. That is, in the privacy of his own room and on his own time he can read the letter. By being in charge of time and setting there is a much greater chance that he will also feel free to take the suggestions that he deems useful—he's less defensive and more open.

Jason,

I know that this has been a rough year for you. For some reason it's been hard to find friends at this new high school. But it'll get better in time. You've had too many good friends for me to think otherwise—Isaac and Phil from summer camp; Tom and Billy from eighth grade; and Lewis from elementary school. Remember how you were elected vice president in seventh grade? Anyway, know that your father and I are very proud of you—both for your accomplishments and for the kind of person you are. We couldn't ask for more. I know you'll have plenty of friends by the end of high school, so just hang in there and never doubt yourself. While I can't help you find friends, I can support you in any way you want, even if it means being quiet. So let me know if there is anything I can do.

I love you,

Mom

Also, and perhaps most important, a letter is a communication of your love and respect for him. It takes time to write a letter, and he appreciates the effort. It also makes him feel that you're on his side without being intrusive, that you actively believe in him. A letter also lasts; kids tend to hold onto these letters and read them over time, similar to old pictures that are saved.

> The other day my son called and asked if I would do a huge favor for him: bring the history paper that was due next period to him at school (he'd forgotten it at home). Well, when I was getting the paper I noticed my handwriting on a piece of paper in his top drawer, so I looked more closely. In the drawer were dozens of brief notes I had given him over the past few years. He had saved all of them! What is most incredible is that at the time he barely even acknowledged getting them. I always assumed he read and tossed them without a second thought!

Finally, notes acknowledge teenagers' struggle without either taking it over or abandoning them in their time of need. This is a tricky and essential line to walk, but as with so much a parent must do, walking this line must become a high art.

CHAPTER 14

The Driver's License

How can we expect our sixteen-year-old daughter to be ready to drive a car when she can't even keep her room clean?

Dr. John Dyckman, a developmental psychologist, states that there are two events in peoples' lives that change their worldview forever. The first is learning to walk. When infants go from crawling to walking, their perspective of and relationship to the world expands dramatically. The ability to walk enhances adventure, strengthens self-determination, and lends efficient mobility to curiosity. The second irrevocable change to one's worldview is getting a driver's license. If walking, and later, riding a bike, represent dramatic changes in mobility, driving a car is exponentially more so. For teenagers, it is especially dramatic because now they also have an expanded sense of consciousness to go along with this newly increased mobility. Adolescents who obtain a driver's license have more independence and more say over what they do and where they go. Conversely, you have less say over what they do and where they go. This is no minor change.

Ideally parents start to consider driving privileges when their child is twelve or thirteen years old. You ask yourself: "What do I need to see from my daughter in terms of responsibility and maturity to feel comfortable with her driving the car in three or four years?" From there you gradually give her more and more responsibilities so that she can mature and gain experience—along the way to the driver's license, not afterwards. My own mother was quite familiar with this kind of forward thinking.

As early as grade school, my mother realized that I needed to slowly learn to take care of myself, so that was when my lessons began. Typically she would meet me after school and fix me a snack, but at times she would not be home (there would be a note) when I arrived home from school. While I was nervous about this, I did learn to fix my own snack and go about my after-school routine. It was only later, as an adult, that I learned that whenever she wasn't home she was across the street at a neighbor's house running from window to window making sure that I was all right! It was in this way that she taught me to manage my anxiety so that later in life—adolescence—when she didn't have such direct control over me, I would be familiar with taking responsibility in the face of anxiety.

Handled this way, turning sixteen and driving aren't such a leap of faith for both parents and teenagers. Otherwise, the possible dangers of driving are justifiably overwhelming for parents. As every parent knows too well, one mistake here can be life-changing and even life-ending, something no parent wants to have to live with.

Even though Josh is a junior, I still refuse to let him drive the car any more than a few miles away on a weekend evening. I'm just so frightened about drunk drivers, never mind the possibility that he might drink and drive. It's really sad, but I'm almost willing to have my son hate me during the next two years in order to ensure his safety. I would rather have a relationship to work on a few years from now than nothing to work with besides grief and guilt. I know I sound ultraconservative, and I don't think I am in most areas, but there is just too much to lose in this area.

Before getting to the pragmatics of driving, let's think about another inevitable conflict it stirs in the parent-adolescent relationship: time spent with one another. As teenagers get older, most parents see them less and less, which is fine with them. In fact, they need to move away from you and toward their friends as a part of the normal development to adulthood, but as far as most parents are concerned they don't need to do it with such glee.

> Ever since Tom started high school, we've been progressively seeing less of him. It began with him being home but preoccupied with phone conversations and homework. Now his friends, who all seem to have their licenses and ready access to cars, get him at nights to "go out" for awhile. We're afraid we'll never see him after he gets his license! It almost feels like he is a boarder now; I can't imagine what it will be like after he gets his license. It's kind of sad for us, but Tom is blind to that part of it; all he can do is count the days until his driving test.

Because the topic of driving brings on significant amounts of anxiety, be as clear as you can on the topic and keep it separate from other issues. Making driving a power issue isn't good for anyone. Rather, make it a process that requires teenagers to behave responsibly (something that is within their control) en route to successfully acquiring the license. Your job is to consult, assess, and possibly help out at appropriate times in the process. In this sense, the driver's license is an invitation to responsibility.

> I know my parents will never let me drive. I'll have to wait until college. I'm serious! Every time I bring it up they're like, "Well, we'll have to see how things are going when the time comes." But when I ask they can never tell me what these "things" are. Then to cinch the deal, whenever I get in any kind of trouble they say that these are the kinds of "things" they're talking about! Of course they never point out or seem to remember any of the good things I do. They're nuts. I'm probably not even going to bug them about it when the time comes; I don't want to give them the satisfaction of holding that power over me.

It's unfair to communicate mixed messages to your teenager and then get mad at her when she gets upset at the mixed messages (and then to use her reaction as an example of why she is not ready for her license!). For instance, who is going to teach her to drive and who is she going to practice driving with? Are you necessarily the right person? At times it makes a great deal of sense to hire a professional if neither parent is honestly up to the task. This is also a good time to put more responsibility back on your teenager. Why should you have to make all the difficult decisions while she gets all the perks? Beat her to the punch: Talk to her about driving on her fifteenth birthday. Tell her what a big deal it is, and encourage her to take control of the process and make it impossible for you to refuse her her license when she turns sixteen. Invite her to create her own plan for getting her license and your approval.

> At the beginning of tenth grade, my parents had a parents-to-daughter chat with me. I knew it had to do with my upcoming sixteenth birthday. Sure enough—but what they had to say was kind of cool. They were putting me in charge of getting my license. Of course, I had to meet their requirements. After impressing upon me how big a deal it was to drive a car, they talked about how it was also very frightening to them. They understood their fear was natural but nonetheless it was there, and as far as they were concerned it was part of my job to keep tabs on their fear and keep it to a minimum. Their requirements were: I could have no sudden drops in grades before or after the license; I would find, enroll in, and complete a certified driver's education course (they would pay); I would talk to the insurance company and get the required paperwork for us to go over together; I would pay for half the insurance adjustment; and I would drive for ten hours with my dad prior to making the appointment for the driver's test (after I'd completed the driver's ed course).

Act as the health and safety consultant on this issue. Separate actions and consequences ahead of time. For instance, no parent wants their teenager to get behind the wheel after drinking or ride in the car of another driver who has been drinking. This is the place for clear structure.

If I ever discover you driving under the influence, that's it; you'll never drive again until you go off to college. No exceptions. However, if you take the car and go out drinking, but get a ride home or call me for a ride, that is a different matter. That, of course, would involve other consequences —but nothing around the car, as you would have been quite responsible about the car in that instance. Understand the difference. Risking your safety unnecessarily is not negotiable.

Along the same lines, a parent recently told me that she leaves twenty dollars in the drawer by the front door for her daughter's emergency taxi fare. If her daughter needs a safe ride home from anywhere at anytime she can call a cab and use the twenty to pay the fare—no questions asked.

Whatever format you agree upon for learning and practicing driving, make sure you stick to it unless you mutually decide otherwise. Remember, by the time teenagers turn sixteen, driving the car is more than just idle daydreaming, so your agreements are important. At the same time, don't rush into the process simply because you don't have the time to think it through. Make the time. After your daughter gets her license you will see less and less of her, but that is the case whether she gets her license or not. Also, there is a small percentage of adolescents (especially in urban areas that have accessible mass-transit systems) who are not interested in obtaining their licenses. There is nothing wrong with them; just give them their space and independence to choose if and when.

The driver's license is not only a real change in lifestyle, but it is also a very symbolic change in your relationship. Society recognizes adolescents as citizens responsible enough to earn the privilege of driving. It won't be long now before your relationship with your daughter will change even more, since graduation and future decisions are just around the corner. Finally, as in all aspects of the parent-adolescent relationship, don't expect perfection on your part or your teenager's part. It'll never happen. The only thing you can honestly do is the best you can. And when you mess up, be forthright about taking responsibility for your behavior. Given the high stakes that accompany the driver's license, you'll mess up somewhere along the way. As always, your modeling is vitally important.

This chapter concludes with an article by writer D.L. Stewart.[1] It will help you both to appreciate the complexity of the driver's license issue and to decide if you are the right person to teach your teenager how to drive.

A Teen's Lesson in Lurching

I know it is going to be a tough afternoon when I explain to the sixteen-year-old that learning to drive a stick-shift car is a simple matter of moving a lever into first, second, third, and fourth gears. And he replies:

"In any particular order?"

Teaching a sixteen-year-old how to master four-on-the-floor is simple. All it takes is the patience of Mother Teresa, the courage of Dave Dravecky, and the neck muscles of Mike Tyson. I don't care how many times you may have been rear-ended, you don't know what whiplash is until you've sat in the passenger seat next to a sixteen-year-old who decides that it would be a good idea to go from third to reverse. Without using the clutch.

But each time another of our kids turns sixteen, their mother tosses me a set of car keys and informs me it's a father's job to teach his child how to operate a stick-shift car.

"Why do I have to do it?" I always whine.

"Because I'm the one who went through labor," she always replies. There's no sense arguing with a woman who has waited sixteen years for revenge.

On the first Sunday after our latest kid hits sixteen she tosses me the car keys again, and I drive him to an empty parking lot that surrounds a football stadium. It is a place that obviously is frequently used by parents teaching their kids to drive. The lot is littered with empty Valium bottles.

I stop in a spot as far away from the stadium as possible. It's not that I don't have complete faith in his driving ability, but it's not a real big stadium and there is always that chance that he might not notice it.

The sixteen-year-old and I trade seats, and I start to explain to him about the clutch and the "rpms" and how the gears are arranged in the figure H.

"I know, Dad, I know," he says, impatiently, pushing in the clutch and stepping on the accelerator. He lets out the clutch, the car lurches forward, bounces twice and shudders to a stop.

"Did I do something wrong?" he asks.

"Don't worry, you'll get the hang of it," I assure him. "Next time give it just a little more gas."

He turns on the ignition, steps on the clutch, shoves the accelerator to the floor and revs the engine. If he pops the clutch now, I realize as the tachometer needle goes through the red zone for the third time, I won't have to worry about us running into the stadium. We'll just catapult over it.

"You might want to ease off on the gas a tiny bit," I suggest, bracing my feet against the dashboard.

He cuts it back to two million rpms and pops the clutch. The car lurches forward, bounces six times and stalls again. When it has finished shuddering, I crawl out of the backseat and rejoin him in the front.

"Sorry about that," he says.

"No big deal," I assure him. "When I was teaching your sister, I wound up in the trunk."

He tries again. This time the car does not lurch. It soars. I'm not sure what kind of mileage this car gets, but it gets great altitude.

"How was it that time?" he asks when we have returned to earth.

"Well, the takeoff wasn't bad, but you need to work on your landings."

After half an hour, we have covered approximately fifty yards. In forty-nine lurches.

On the other hand, I've got to give the kid credit. It's not often you get to drive with someone who can stop a car forty-nine consecutive times without ever using the brakes.

Endnote

1. D. L. Stewart, "On Being a Dad: A Teen's Lesson in Lurching."

❧ CHAPTER 15 ❦

Eating Modifications and Eating Disorders

My daughter, who is on the slim side, seems to be eating less and less these days, and I think she is losing weight. What is going on?

The questions here are, "Does my daughter have an eating disorder?" or, more specifically, "How do I tell if my daughter has an eating disorder?" and, "If she does have an eating disorder, what can I do about it?" There is no simple answer to any of these questions; it is indeed a tricky area for both parents and educators. On the one hand, many parents think:

> It is best not to say anything until I am absolutely sure, as I don't want to offend my daughter and inadvertently alienate her. Maybe it's just a passing thing, and if I ignore it it'll go away—kind of like when she was seeing that awful Bobby G. I held back on that one, and sure enough, she dropped him of her own volition. Besides, she is growing quite a bit, so perhaps I'm overreacting. I'll wait until I'm sure.

But, on the other hand:

> I must confront her on this right now. If I ignore it it'll only get worse, and I'll be ignoring my responsibilities as her mother. Not only that, but I have to get her to a therapist as

> soon as possible. Or at least we have to make an agreement
> on her eating so that I can keep track of how she is doing.

The problem is that neither of these two strategies is typically successful. Ignoring the problem and hoping that it'll go away is often worth a short-term attempt, but if an eating disorder is the problem, other strategies are called for. Also, by the time the parent notices it, a problem with eating has probably been going on quite a while. Parents are typically the last to notice, for two reasons. First, you are around your daughter every day, so the gradual loss of weight over time is difficult to notice. Second, since you don't want to see this happen to your child, your natural tendency will be to not notice it. [1]

Where do eating disorders come from and what are they all about? Bulimia and anorexia are the two most common disorders. Bulimia is characterized by self-induced vomiting and/or the overuse of diuretics, typically after gorging or "binging" on food. Binging comes about after short periods of starvation or extreme dieting, and is often thought of as a lack of will, which is "made right" through vomiting. In this misery-go-round, not only do bulimics do themselves harm but they also feel bad about themselves for having succumbed to the binging behavior. Bulimia erodes its victim's self-confidence and developing personal identity.

Anorexia is a distortion of a person's self-image that leads to self-starvation. It can, but need not, be accompanied by bulimic behavior. Anorexia is also frequently accompanied by rigid and extreme exercise, often running and aerobics. Most frightening of all, the most frequent victims of these two eating disorders are bright, creative, talented, and motivated adolescent girls: in short, the kind of kid every parent dreams of having.

During high school, a fair number of teenagers flirt with eating modifications of one variety or another—usually during their freshman and sophomore years. At first, such behavior is quite seductive and gives them a sense of accomplishment and control, a crucial counterpoint to the frequent out-of-control feelings of adolescence.

> I'm not bulimic or anything, but I've experimented with
> making myself throw up. I hated it! Still though, every once

in a while I'll go a few days where I hardly eat anything, mostly to lose a few pounds (which I know doesn't work!) but also to feel better about myself. It is like I prove to myself that I am in control and that I do have strong will-power. I can see how it could become addictive.

There is also the notion (supported by media images and cultural values) that "thinner is better," and that by becoming thinner, adolescents also become more attractive and popular. This idea is reinforced by the attention they get when losing weight.

Lots of people noticed and complimented me, including some people I hardly even knew. Even my father noticed and said something positive, which really threw me! It was kind of funny, though; even though I was getting all this attention, it didn't make any difference in the long run. My standards were so much higher than everyone else's.

Parents need to be thoughtful about the messages they give their adolescents regarding food and weight. "Playfully" teasing girls about getting fat because they are having a piece of cake can be harmful. They are already quite self-conscious, and your teasing only magnifies those feelings, no matter how benevolent the intention.

I wish I could tell my mom how much it hurts me when she comments or gives me a raised eyebrow when I eat dessert. I imagine her heart is in the right place, but it sure feels awful.

Finally, in the adolescent world of ambiguity and rapid change, weight is something that can be controlled as it is tangible and measurable. They can and do regularly assess themselves with a high degree of accuracy.

The scale never lies. Every morning when I wake up, I weigh myself to see if my weight has changed. If I've lost even a little bit I'm in a great mood. If I haven't changed at all I'm pretty medium. But if I've gained even a little bit I get real angry with myself and make plans [by exercising and not eating] to lose the weight by the end of the day.

Also, as weight and food become a greater focus in a teenager's life, she may focus all her anxiety on weight rather than on the more ambiguous but necessary issues of adolescence—see Chapters 2 and 3 for examples of these issues.

> After a while all I could think about was food: what I had and had not eaten already during the day, what I would or wouldn't eat next, and how I would eat tomorrow. I even began saying yes or no to social engagements based on food. If it was a get-together around dinner I always said no, but if it was just for coffee I was fine. I definitely wasn't interested in alcohol or drugs—I was afraid of losing control and binging. It pretty much took over my life. Because I was so focused on food, I blocked out all sorts of other concerns and worries that I would otherwise have to face daily—like getting close friends, having sex, and most of all, figuring out what I want to do with my life and who I want to be.

So, what do you do if you suspect your teenager has an eating disorder? Asking her directly sometimes works, but just as often ends with the feeling of having run into a brick wall.

> When I confronted her with her eating habits she looked at me like I was from another planet. She gave me a look that sent a shiver down my spine and simply dismissed the subject! I haven't brought it up since.

Instead, set the context for asking the question. Specifically, you need to understand that this is a disease that is taking or has already taken over; it is *not* a sign of weakness nor a matter of willpower. When you speak with your daughter, she needs to understand and feel that you are not accusing her of any wrongdoing. If you can create this environment, many adolescents will be fairly honest with you, even somewhat relieved. Some parents have had success with writing letters to their teenager voicing their concern and support. Then, when they have the conversation, the groundwork has already been laid.

> At first I wanted my not eating to be my own secret, but when it got out of control I wanted to tell my parents so they could help me. But I just couldn't bring myself to tell them directly. It would have been too humiliating. So what I did was give them all sorts of hints (telling them all about my exercise, not eating with them because I didn't feel hungry, wearing tight clothes that showed how thin I was, and telling them how some people were commenting on how much weight I had lost) so that they finally had to ask me. Even then I acted angry with them when they asked me about it, but eventually I did tell them.

In fact, by the time the amount of food intake has changed, the disorder is probably comfortably settled in with your teenager. So as she recovers, the last thing to change will probably be her food habits.

> Once I told my parents that I was anorexic, they completely panicked and misunderstood what I said. Sure, they were supportive, which was nice, but they were also pretty naive about what I needed. Asking me daily about what I ate, making lunches for me to take to school, and insisting that I eat dinner with them were all counterproductive. The anorexia was so strong in me that when they asked about what I ate, it [the anorexia] got me to lie. I gave the wonderful lunches to street people on my way to school. And eating in front of my parents only made me resort to throwing up afterwards.

Think of an eating disorder in the same way you would any other disease that might infect your child. If your daughter was lethargic and sleeping all the time, you wouldn't ask her if she had mononucleosis. You would take her to the doctor. Do the same with eating disorders—accurate and honest self-diagnosis is rare. Immediately alert your physician to your fears. Then, if this is an area your physician is comfortable addressing, set up an appointment for your daughter to have a physical. The physician should be able to spot signs of anorexia and bulimia and make a reliable diagnosis. From there, if an eating disorder is diagnosed, a treatment plan can be formulated, mainly between the physician and the adolescent. Parents typically play an adjunct role in treatment, which often includes some form of psychotherapy.

> The doctor was good with my daughter, and even better with me. It took a while, but she finally convinced my husband and me that it would be best if we didn't bring up the topic of food with Susan. She said to leave that to her and the therapist. We were to be supportive and loving of Susan as a person and to hold her accountable as we would any other young adult. She also told us that we might be asked to attend her counseling sessions periodically, but that we should wait for the invitation. She was immensely helpful to all of us.

I have used the female pronoun in this chapter because 90 percent of adolescents suffering from eating disorders are female. Probably the closest parallel with male adolescents is bodybuilding carried to an extreme. Overdeveloped muscles construct an emotional armor around boys, just as anorexia creates an emotional fog around its victims. And rather than self-starvation, the drug of choice is frequently steroids.

A useful way to conceptualize an eating disorder comes from New Zealand therapist David Epston and Australian therapist Michael White, who view an eating disorder as a separate entity that is attempting to take over the body and personality of the host. This is also a very useful way to discuss this issue with teenagers, as it pits them in a fight against an external agent rather than an internal part of themselves. They can eventually reclaim themselves from the foreign entity without sacrificing a part of themselves. Moreover, this is how the eating disorder is experienced by the victim. The following is a sample of the type of letter I might give to a teenager suffering from anorexia.

Dear _____,

From our conversation it is clear that you are now making a stand against the tyranny of anorexia in your life. You also understand that this is both a lengthy and arduous process. To this extent you need all the support you can muster, which also means separating, on a deep level, what supports you as a person and what inadvertently supports the anorexia. You've discovered that this is not so obvious as it seems at first glance.

Clearly you want your parents' full support, but past efforts have failed to claim that necessary support. You've insisted on nonfat foods, avoided family obligations that have centered on dining, exercised fanatically within their plain view, and still have not gotten the attention you need from them. Further, you visited a physician in an attempt to get the subject out in the open with your parents, but that failed miserably because all he did was focus on the vegetarianism and refer you to a nutritionist—as if you need any outside assistance in monitoring your eating habits!

Even though your skin is slightly jaundiced, your wrists are tiny, your hair is beginning to fall out, and you've lost 20 pounds over the past six months, nobody seems willing to recognize what is going on. They all want to look the other way in the hopes that it's "just a phase." Which was probably a suitable strategy in the beginning, but you are now way beyond the beginning. On top of this, what notice your parents have paid to the anorexia has resulted in a lot of mixed messages: Your mom is upset with your exclusively nonfat diet, but she reprimands you for eating a taco with cheese and sour cream! Your dad is worried about the amount you exercise, but compliments you on how good you look. (To this end, you've sadly recognized how "thin beauty" has taken over the typical American mind—especially in men.)

You fear that if you do muster the strength to tell your parents you have anorexia, you'll inadvertently invite them in as "food monitors," a possibility that you understandably dread. You really liked what happened with Karen and her anorexia. Once her disease was recognized, she started seeing a therapist and her physician. The therapist was someone she liked and with whom she simply talked about her life's events and seldom directly discussed food. The physician she met with asked only about the anorexia. He was very firm and had a clear weight in mind, that, if Karen dropped to it, would automatically land her in the hospital for at least a month, and Karen knew he wasn't kidding. Further, you especially liked that he forbade her family, and especially her parents, to ever talk to her about food or the anorexia. In fact, he insisted that Karen eat what, where, and when she liked. Her parents could never insist that she join them for dinner or for any other meal. Only he, the physician, would discuss food and eating with her. And yes, this was the person with whom she was brash, pouty, rude, and outspoken—all without feeling guilty!

Your friends. You need them now more than ever, but you understand how hard you are to access and how paralyzed they feel. The anorexia, gradually taking root in your thinking, has created this fog all around you that literally leaves you a step behind in conversations and misperceiving all that is happening around you. In fact, the coldness of the fog encourages you to retreat further into your own world and the world of anorexia, which is compulsive in its focus on food, grams of fat, calories, and future planning for food. However, once your friends had gotten over their shyness about the food and focused on their concern for you, they tried to be supportive. While you didn't like them offering you food and encouraging you to eat, you did appreciate their intentions. And you understood why, with no results, they stopped offering the encouragement. You felt somewhat abandoned, but not able to tell them clearly what you needed: their unconditional love and support throughout this ordeal, even though they wouldn't be able to help directly. If only you could have gotten them to view the anorexia as a kind of long-term pneumonia. Anyway, they've gotten discouraged, and with the distancing effects of the anorexia they have drifted away from you.

Your teachers. Oddly, this has been the best support system you've had to date. Unexpectedly, Mrs. Nelson recognized what was going on with you and spoke her concerns and support to you directly. It was a great relief for someone to recognize what was happening without your having to tell them. Further, she was not afraid to talk about it with you and seemed very understanding and non-judgmental. In fact, it was the relationship with her that encouraged you to squarely address the anorexia by coming to my office to get some ideas and the names of some local therapists. Quite a step.

We left our conversation with the idea of deciding how to alert your parents to the situation without further strengthening the anorexia. We discussed several options: you could write them a letter (as conversation often goes down undesirable but seemingly unavoidable paths); we could invite them into my office so you could tell them here; or we could invite them into my office, without your presence, so I could catch them up. It is now in your hands. While you want all the support you can get, you also fully understand that only you can make this stand against anorexia. You call the shots as to when, where, and how.

That is where we ended yesterday. Since then, however, I've thought of a few more questions I wished I had asked when you were here. I thought to include them, as they might assist you in determining your next step.

How did you manage to overcome the paralyzing effects of anorexia to voluntarily come into my office to enlist my help? You attribute much to Mrs. Nelson, but I suspect there is more. For instance, were you valuing yourself differently in order to make such a dramatic move? And if so, how were you valuing yourself differently? And how did you manage to do this in the presence of the anorexia?

See you soon.

Mike

Endnote

1. As with alcohol and drug abuse, if you are concerned that your adolescent may have an eating disorder, you need to contact a professional as well as get up-to-date information on the problem. An eating disorder is not simply a matter of home management.

CHAPTER 16

Adolescent Grieving

*Is there a normal grieving process for
teenagers who have suffered the death
of a parent or other loved one?*

The death of a loved one is an emotional catastrophe that cannot be minimized or rationalized, and it is something experienced by many teenagers. How this grief is handled is both an individual matter and also a somewhat known process, much the same as for adults. However, the competing horizons of adolescence, along with the interdependence of family members, make teenagers especially vulnerable to the death of a loved one. Particularly with the death of a parent, the adolescent is affected not only by a significant emotional loss but also by a change in family responsibility and day-to-day life.

> After my father died, my relationship with my mom became much more grown-up. We had to talk about real issues with each other: responsibilities around the house, finances, and the behavior of my little sister in school. Mom was still the mom and I was still the son, but we were also different. We had to trust each other more. She had to work a lot and as a result I assumed more responsibility around the house. I began to cook many of the meals and to do some of the shopping. It was kind of weird at first, but I'm glad she turned to me like that, even if it was out of desperation.

There are definitely stages to grief. (Writer Elizabeth Kübler-Ross identifies five stages: denial, anger, bargaining, depression, and acceptance.) However, these stages are not experienced discreetly or linearly. People cycle through these stages at various rates, sometimes getting stuck in one or completely skipping over another. There is no orderly process to grief, especially with the volatile nature of adolescence (see Chapter 2).

> It took me a long time to really believe that Sharon [a friend killed in an accident] had died. I simply didn't want to believe it. I couldn't handle it. It was a while ago, and while I've been very depressed and angry at times, there are still lots of moments when I don't believe it. It's kind of weird; sometimes I have to make myself remember that she is dead.

But given the nature of death, ambiguity is a part of the grieving process—it is difficult to know what to think or feel. This ambiguity is often rough on teenagers, who are relatively inexperienced with such concepts. On the other hand, they don't have old coping mechanisms that bog them down. Either way, ambiguity causes behavior that must be acknowledged, especially in mood changes.

> For at least the first few months [after her sister's death] I was all over the map. Sometimes I would go from laughing with friends to all of a sudden crying. I mean really crying and sobbing uncontrollably. It really freaked us all out at first! Other times I would have this chip on my shoulder, sort of looking for something or someone to get angry at. And sometimes I had so much energy I couldn't sleep, while other times I could hardly get out of bed. But the worst for me was that I couldn't make a decision about anything! I was so indecisive that I drove myself crazy! The worst was one day at a pizza place when I broke down crying because I couldn't decide what toppings I wanted on my pizza. Thank God my friends were with me.

While there is more or less a pattern to the grief process, it is also quite individual. There are no rigid rights or wrongs. Some teenagers will talk and emote a great deal; others get very physical (especially through sports); and others go more or less into seclusion. Some become very focused on one area of their life (academics, sports, music); and some make an abrupt change in their lifestyle. One observation I've made is that often adolescents react by making their world smaller. That is, they turn their attention and focus to one or two things that suddenly emerge from their usual variety of activities. This shrinking of their world gives them a greater sense of control in the face of an uncontrollable event, and is often a healthy and useful response.

> After my mom died it was pretty strange. Everything was unreal. But shortly afterward I got very focused on my schoolwork. It became a real priority for me, and as a result I dropped some of my other interests...for all that year I got better grades than ever before. It was the opposite of what everyone expected, including me.

Or,

> At first, after Dad died, I hated being by myself; I always wanted people around me. And I talked to everybody about how I felt. But then, a few weeks after the funeral, I just wanted to be alone. I pushed everyone away except my two closest friends. But even with them I hardly talked about my dad. For some reason I just wanted to be alone most of the time. I was no longer interested in what my friends were interested in; it all seemed so superficial. Besides, I wanted my life to be less complicated, not more complicated.

How a teenager reacts to death is attributable to a number of interrelated variables: his relationship to the deceased, his prior experience with death, the type of death (sudden or prolonged), the reactions of those around him, the reactions of his friends to him, and his basic personality. However he deals with his grief, it is a long-term process (and longer the closer the person was to him). It is not something that he simply goes through and beyond in a few weeks or months. It becomes a sedimented part of his past; when other loved ones die, the previous death is recalled as both an experience and as a process of grief. (See Diagram 1: Stress Buffer Zone on page 28.)

So, what is helpful? Time and persistent invitations to conversation. Give him all the time you can, be it quietly tagging along on errands, helping with tasks around the house, or going to shows and games together. And while you give him time, don't be offended when he says "no." Let it be OK, but don't let it stop you from asking again in the future. Talk to him about what happened, and don't try to take away his anxiety or sadness. Also, don't insist upon anxiety or sadness.

> A month or so after my sister [Cheryl] died, I was on a walk with my dad. At one point his voice got a little high-pitched and he said he wanted to talk about talking about Cheryl. He didn't want to force anything on me but he wanted the subject to always be open between us. He didn't want to turn a deaf ear to me or make me talk about Cheryl. It was kind of scary, because I realized that he was as confused as I was. But at least we had each other, which helped quite a bit.

Also, realize that for quite awhile he will be going through an internal reorganization.

> I really didn't think my father's death [in the eighth grade] affected me that much—until right before high school graduation, when I looked back on my high school career. Then it was totally obvious. It was like my life was headed in one direction and, when he died, it suddenly shifted into another direction. Not better or worse, just different. It was pretty amazing to realize.

And,

> Even though my brother died in the spring, that first Christmas was a real hard time. It was very sad and felt hollow. I got pretty cynical about all holidays after that. [1]

Understand that for most people the major effects of the death of a loved one usually begin a couple of months after the death. Prior to that, most people are so overwhelmed by the event and the concern of others that they don't have the time or space to do their own processing. Be sure to check in with your teenager after a few months, when talk and companionship are most helpful and useful.

> When my dad died we [the family] got all this immediate attention and sympathy from friends, neighbors, and family. And the food! Everyone we ever met must have brought us meals during that first month. It was all quite amazing, so much so that it was hard for anything to sink in. It wasn't until a few months later that my dad's death really hit me. All of a sudden my family and I were developing a routine that didn't include my father. It was like there was this giant empty hole in everything we did. Those months were by far the hardest. And of course by then everybody had gone on with their lives and had stopped talking with me about my dad. I didn't see the empty void until all the support was gone, so I had to deal with it alone, which was pretty much a drag.

You should also be aware of the periodic appearance of "red flags" that are insistent invitations for your intervention in your teenager's grieving process. He may become overwhelmed and self-destructive in some manner, whether blatant or subtle: skipping school (sometimes bordering on dropping out), getting heavily into drugs or alcohol, or becoming violent toward others (fighting) or himself (suicide). (See Chapter 21 for more on this topic.) These are signs that health and safety are at issue. You must intervene directly and may have to enlist the support of others, including a professional counselor.

> For awhile after my mother died I was pretty crazy. I would get drunk and do anything on a dare: walk on a high ledge, steal booze from a liquor store, drive incredibly fast, or talk back in class (when I went). Finally, a couple of teachers, my soccer coach, and my dad all sat down and confronted me with what I was doing. It was a pretty ugly scene. I didn't

cop to anything. But in the end my dad and I both went to a shrink for awhile, often together. It also helped my dad, as he wasn't doing much better than me. I think I would be dead otherwise, or at least thrown out of my house.

As odd as it sounds and no matter how difficult the course, adolescents are very resilient and with time they develop strength and resources from having to deal with this type of hardship, as long as they are allowed to move at their own pace. Most people who have endured hardships of one kind or another will say that suffering made them stronger and gave them more depth.

Finally, in discussing the death of a loved one with students, I find it is frequently useful for them to work through this process in their own time (without feeling abandoned), with the implicit message that they are capable of handling this and that you trust them. They also need to discern how to move on with their lives without forgetting the person who died. I often give a variation of the following letter to teenagers to take home and read at their leisure, and to reread over time. In this example, the letter references the death of the teenager's mother.

Dear _____,

In trying to come to grips with the death of a loved one, people often speak of "letting go" and "moving on," which are all said with the best intentions. People want to see you whole again, happy again, and living your life fully again. However, there is also the underlying message that this person is dead, the relationship is over, and that life is for the living. While this is quite true, it is also not the entire story.

When your mother was alive, you had a relationship with her that was important and vital to you. With her death it feels like the relationship has died along with her, even though the relationship need not die. To "get on with your life" and "let go of your grief" you may need to first form another relationship with her that replaces the old relationship. Your mother was too important to you to simply forget about, and many people won't or can't "move on" until they are sure that they won't forget. But the process of creating this new relationship is seldom spoken of, even though it is common sense. You see, the new relationship is one in which you bring your mother into yourself, into your imagination if you wish. You create a small space within yourself for her, a place that you can reference whenever you wish. Believe me, this is not as crazy as it seems at first glance.

You knew your mom quite well, well enough to know how she would respond to certain situations and certain questions. You knew how she acted and felt when you misbehaved. You knew how to please her. You also knew how to tease her, make her laugh, and anger her. There are many more general and idiosyncratic things that you knew about her that occur to you whenever you think of her. And there are many more things you knew about her that perhaps you don't yet remember. That is part of the purpose of this letter; to help you remember some of the aspects of your mom that you knew so well in a manner that allows the essence of her to remain within you. You can have an active and changing memory of her in the present versus a passive and stagnant memory of her in the past.

With the above in mind, take some time to reflect on the following questions. You may want to come back to these questions at various times. You will probably also come up with some of your own questions that help create a living memory of your mom. Do whatever is most helpful to you. (However, if you do come up with some new questions that are useful to you, please pass them on to me so that they can be incorporated into this letter for others to use.)

What are some of your favorite mental snapshots of your mom? What do you imagine are some of her favorite mental snapshots of you? How about of the two of you together?

When did she surprise you by something she said or did? How did this increase your understanding and appreciation of her? And, how did you surprise her by something you said or did? What did this tell her about you that she didn't know before?

Is there any particular song, book, poem, or art piece that you associate with her? If not, think of one now. What about that represents her to you, and what aspect of her does it represent?

What did she see in you that was special? How did she communicate this to you? And how did you let her know that you got it?

I hope these questions help in the building of a new relationship with your mother, one that keeps her alive within you, and you alive within her.

Best wishes,

Mike

Endnote

1. As holidays and anniversaries are difficult for many adolescents (see Chapter 17 for more on the effects of holidays on adolescents), University High School sponsors a "holiday blues group" during the major holiday season. By talking, telling stories, and reinventing traditions, participants "sing" themselves and one another through to the other side of the holiday funk.

Divorce

How does divorce affect a teenager?

Just as there is no one common adult experience of divorce, there is also no universal adolescent experience of divorce. Divorce is one of those phenomena that dominates (as it should) the landscape of the teenager during and intermittently before and after the actual divorce. Before, the adolescent can usually feel what is coming—I've rarely spoken to a teenager who was genuinely surprised, no matter how discreet the parents were.

> I knew they were going to get divorced before they ever said anything to me. There are lots of signs if you just look: hushed conversations when I walked into the room, tearful phone conversations, late-night arguments, separate bank accounts, and in general, lots of haggard and exhausted looks.

Teenagers react to this in a variety of ways. Some try to make things better between their parents by being nice and supportive to both of them—they hope that somehow if they are good, their parents will become more peaceful and loving with one another. They create the illusion of control, that they can keep the family together if they just are good enough.[1] Others, feeling the lack of consistency and attention at home, begin to act out in a variety of ways: getting heavily into the party scene, slacking off in school, arguing with teachers and coaches, or becoming depressed. Adolescents must face reality: They are essentially powerless to do anything about the impending divorce, and this is stressful.

During the actual divorce process, most teenagers are somewhat overwhelmed and confused by the divorce and by adolescence. How they handle this varies quite a bit, but their behavioral changes are often an extension and escalation of their past behaviors. Some become lost in confusion and act without thinking. Here, one sees an increase in self-destructive and depressive behavior: appetite changes, sleep problems, and a general lack of motivation.

> When my parents were getting divorced, it was pretty crazy around my house. They were arguing so much with each other that they kind of forgot about me. You know, nobody checked on my curfew and they pretty much let me do whatever I pleased. It wasn't that they trusted me anymore than before; I just think they didn't have the energy. Anyway, I spent most of that year partying and just hanging out. I did awful in school and in sports, too. It was a real drag. Actually, I was pretty crazy then in some of the things I got into...

Others make their worlds more manageable by making them smaller (see Chapter 16). Here one sees the adolescent get very focused on one area of life: sports, academics, a relationship, a theatrical production at school.

> When my parents split up, I was a junior in high school. Up until that point I had been just a fair guitar player. I had taken lessons for a few years, but had never really gotten into it. Well, during the divorce I picked up the guitar again and got into it like I never had before. I took lessons, practiced with a vengeance, played CDs over and over again, hooked up with a band, and even began writing my own music. I probably spent three to four hours every weeknight, and more on weekends, playing guitar during my junior year. I definitely didn't do any homework! There was no way I could concentrate on schoolwork, but I sure could focus on the guitar. It was a real escape for me, a place where I didn't have to think about anything.

However it is manifested, the divorce significantly undoes the home foundation that is so necessary for the teenager to cope with all the inevitable changes and decisions of adolescence. As one sophomore who was struggling with her personal identity once told me in the midst of her parents' divorce: "How can I find myself when everything around me is going crazy?"

After the divorce, things hopefully settle down, with both the parents and the teenager coming to conscious grips with the realities of their new worlds. But this process doesn't happen overnight; it generally takes at least a year. The analogy I use with students is that the psychic and emotional injuries from the divorce are similar to seriously breaking a leg. If you break your leg badly you can expect an operation and a short hospitalization. When you get back home, your movements are limited by a cast and crutches for three to six months. Then you can expect several more months of physical therapy. If everything goes exceedingly well you could be back to normal in a year or so. But during that year of recovery, you would significantly scale back your goals and expectations. You would drop certain activities. You would also expect a short-term drop in grades because of the hospitalization and the subsequent lack of durable concentration. You would be sleeping more—because of both the body's healing process and the extra effort required to get around with a cast and crutches. And you could expect lots of attention and sympathy from your peers and family who would constantly inquire about your leg—after all, everybody knows how to support someone with a broken leg. There would be lots of "Get Well" cards, books, crossword puzzles, rented movies, and the like to keep your spirits up during your recovery.

When a family goes through a divorce, it is a similar sort of injury, except that the injury is psychic and emotional instead of physical. Further, people don't know about the injury (divorce) unless you tell them, which isn't easy for even the healthiest of teenagers. With the hyper-self-consciousness of adolescence, it is exceedingly difficult to make oneself voluntarily vulnerable to peers, which unfortunately is the only way to get the healing support of friends for the "divorce injury." Also, because of the relative invisibility of the divorce, others (teachers and coaches) may misinterpret behaviors inaccurately: apathy, disrespect, carelessness, lack of motivation. One of the best things a parent can do for their teenager during the divorce process is to call the school and confidentially let a trusted teacher, coach, or advisor know enough of what is happening at home so they can make sense of any sudden behavioral shifts. You want someone at the school who can act as translator for some of your adolescent's behaviors.

> As Dean of Students, I find it very helpful to hear from parents when their son or daughter is dealing with a traumatic event like an extended illness in the family, the death of a loved one, or divorce. I can then confidentially let the teachers in the school know that the adolescent is going through a difficult time, without having to divulge any of the details. Unless teachers have a close relationship with the student, I ask them not to mention it to the student until he or she brings it up. This way, teachers won't misinterpret a sudden change in the student's behavior.

So what is helpful in assisting a teenager through a divorce? Clearly there is no ideal scenario, as divorce is the result of a failed ideal. You must simply do your best with what is at hand. For now, I'll focus on what I believe are some of the essentials.

While all adolescents are familiar with the concept of divorce (through friends and the media), don't overestimate their knowledge of what divorce actually means; the vocabulary, rights, choices, and responsibilities are often foreign to them.[2] It is helpful to directly answer questions for your kids as well as to find out what they need to know: a timeline for the divorce, details about living arrangements, school changes, financial changes, and the role of their input. Even though you may have this conversation with your adolescent, realize that she'll forget much of it, so expect to repeat it later—she is on overload too. This information serves as a structure for her; it gives her an idea of how to make sense of what follows, as well as a sense of an official end to the divorce proceedings.

Since the divorce process is overwhelming for all concerned, it's sometimes wise to acquire a "divorce consultant" whom your teenager can call or see when she has questions. It can be a friend of the family familiar with divorce logistics, an attorney or mediator hired for a couple of hours, a therapist, or perhaps the counselor or health educator at school. Your adolescent simply needs a place where she can get reliable information and support from a neutral source. She may or may not make use of it, but the important point is that someone is in place for her should she ever need it. Finally, having someone in place for your teenager gives you some peace of mind as well as the room to take better care of yourself and attend to the divorce in a more responsible manner, which ultimately is in everyone's best interest.

In any divorce, consistency is crucial but virtually impossible. Still, as much as possible, parents need to give consistent and reinforced messages to their adolescent, with appropriate follow-through .

> It's weird. Since my parents' divorce, I like it when they are strict with me. I used to yell and scream whenever they were strict, but now I get upset when they aren't. If they let me manipulate them too much I get pissed. I mean they have to do their jobs as parents too.

The little things matter a great deal, such as who is picking your daughter up after school, where and when you are meeting, and in which home she is spending the night. Even though consistent information is tough to come by, because information is constantly changing, be consistent in passing the updated information along.

While teenagers can't be protected from the divorce process (nor should they be) they shouldn't be required to play superior roles either. Most kids fear that they'll have to choose between Mom and Dad, a choice they could never live with within themselves. For them, it is a question of divided loyalty; internally they feel compelled to keep the loyalty split at roughly fifty-fifty. At some point you'll probably encounter what I call the "defensive/empathetic phenomena," which occurs after you have implicitly or explicitly disparaged the other parent:

> ***Mother:*** Your father will pick you up after school today, so don't panic if he isn't waiting for you; you know how he's always late.

Daughter: Mom! Dad is not always late. And when he is, which is less and less these days, he always has a good reason and says he's sorry.

Mother: No, he isn't getting better at being on time. I had to wait twenty minutes at the lawyer's for him the other day! He simply forgets.

Daughter: He does not forget! Why don't you give him a break. He is real busy at work, what with everyone making all sorts of ridiculous demands on him. You could relax a little, you know.

Mother: I can't believe this. Are you the same girl who insisted that I pick you up after last week's dance because you didn't want to be embarrassed by having to stand on the corner to wait for your late father?

In this vignette, the daughter feels compelled to defend her father in his absence (just as she would feel compelled to defend her mother in her absence). What is unfortunate about this is that the daughter gets so busy defending and watching over the fifty-fifty split that she doesn't have time to discern her own feelings and opinions, which is what she most needs to do to move through and beyond the divorce.

Your adolescent must determine her own relationship with each parent, and you must let this happen. Unduly trying to influence the relationship will only come back to haunt you. As your teenager gets older (regardless of when the divorce occurred), she will naturally have more questions about the divorce that need to be addressed. As her thinking changes (see Chapter 2), she needs to reconsider the divorce in light of her new cognitive abilities. As with any traumatic event involving family, you can expect these questions and general issues about the divorce to resurface during the holidays.

Thanksgiving and Christmas really suck since my parents divorced [five years ago]. I know they're [holidays] supposed to be relaxing, fun, peaceful and all that, but that just isn't the way it is. It all starts about a week before Thanksgiving, when my sister and I have to decide where we're going to spend Thanksgiving and Christmas. Each of our parents gets one day, which is better than a few years ago when we spent half a day at each house. A person can eat only so much turkey in one day! No matter what we decide, someone is upset. And then during dinner it is so phony. Everyone just tries so hard to be one happy family that we're all miserable. I can't wait until college, because there is no way I'm coming back for the holidays!

The structure of the final divorce agreement goes a long way toward establishing consistency. Your teenager, through the formal agreement with the courts and the less formal, logistical agreements between parents (with as much input as the adolescent can handle) knows now what to expect. This can be further reinforced. First, he should at least have his own space, even if it means rearranging the house each time he stays there. Second, while some packing and unpacking of things for visits to either parent is necessary, keep it to a minimum. As much as possible, make sure his room is complete. He shouldn't have to bring the alarm clock from apartment to apartment, or his entire wardrobe, or his piano. Ideally he packs his favorite clothes, books, and music. It especially helps if you recognize the stress factor of having to pack up several times a week by purchasing him some luggage or overnight bags that he likes. Finally, it is a pain to have to pack up once or twice a week, so expect some ramifications in unpredictable manners from time to time.

My husband and I divorced when Jackson was seven. For the most part it was an amicable divorce, with the two of us remaining friendly and supportive of one another. We've had joint custody of Jackson the entire time. In fact, we hadn't discussed the divorce in years until one day it came out of the blue, staring me right in the face. I was downstairs preparing to go to work when I heard this loud thud from my son's room. I ran upstairs and saw him despondently sitting on his bed. He looked at me and said through held-back tears, "Sorry, I threw my shoe at the door." I asked, "Why?" To which he replied, "Because the other shoe is at Dad's."

Also expect some settling-in and settling-out time on either end of stays in your home. While you are awaiting your daughter's arrival and setting an extra plate for her, she is packing, saying goodbye, checking her bags, and reminding friends to call her at the other house. You both are preparing to make adjustments to different routines, so simple greeting and good-bye rituals go a long way.

> Every time I go to my mom's, the first thing we do is sit down in the kitchen and have a cup of tea. We each have our regular cups. We catch each other up on our weeks and check in on any plans during the next few days. Sometimes it lasts ten minutes, and other times an hour or so. It's a nice way to get started with each other.

You may as well consciously create these rituals; otherwise they'll simply develop on their own, and won't be nearly as enjoyable.

> Most of the time, on the rides back and forth between Mom's house and Dad's house, I have a big fight with who-ever is driving me. Then I go into the other's house and can't talk to them for a while because I'm too upset at the other one, which of course gets them upset at the other one and leaves me having to defend them even though I'm also upset with them...kind of confusing, huh?

Leave room for negotiation, especially from the teenage perspective, in the divorce settlement. Let your teenager influence the logistics when what she suggests makes common sense. If she has to take the S.A.T.s on Saturday at school and your ex-wife lives next to the school and you live ten miles away, let her negotiate with you and her mother to stay with Mom on that night if she wants. The same for vacations and other trips. You want the spirit of the agreement to be met, which at times will differ from the letter. Also, as she gets older she should have more influence over these decisions. And don't use guilt against her when she finally decides to skip a vacation or holiday with you. Support her and her growing decision-making abilities.

It was so difficult during Karen's junior year when she said that she wanted to live with her father during her senior year. [He lives in the next state and she spends summers with him.] Obviously I was very upset. I felt like somehow he had beaten me. I talked to lots of divorced friends about this. They finally convinced me. So when Karen brought it up to me again I said I would do whatever she wanted. I said I thought it was a good idea for her to get to know her father better and, besides, it would give us some practice for college. I just insisted that she spend the summer before college with me. I also told her that I would really miss her. That was four years ago. From this perspective it's clear that I made the right decision. She and I are very close now, and I can see that if I had fought her on the idea of living with her father we would have had a bloody war that would have taken years to recover from. Thank goodness I had good friends around me.

Finally, for some parents going through the throes of divorce, it is a near-irresistible temptation to use your adolescent as a support and confidante, at times verging on a therapist's role. This is unfair to both of you. Keep her apprised of what she needs to know, but there is no reason to air dirty laundry. Know the difference. This only puts her in the middle and forces her into a defensive position. She is basically in a lose-lose situation. She is grown-up enough to observe and make decisions on her own, but not so grown-up that she can serve as your main support system, especially when it is as a support against her other parent. As much as possible, allow your kid to be a kid. The very nature of divorce forces her to grow up faster than her peers; don't accelerate this process by expecting her to be anything more than a teenager.

The other day I was at a friend's and his mom reminded him that it was his father's birthday the next day. Of course, he had forgotten. But her reminder saved his butt so he could get his dad a present in time and not have to feel like a jerk the next day. Neither my mom or dad would ever do this for me. In fact, I think they hope that I forget the other's birthday. It's sad. It's also kind of unfair that I have to be so responsible all on my own.

As the divorce forces kids to grow up faster, it also gives them more things to think and worry about. Often, these worries affect their sleep patterns; this disruption is the last thing they need. In this regard I often offer the "Putting Your Worries to Bed" technique for teenagers who for one reason or another are unable to fall asleep.

Putting Your Worries to Bed

1. Comfortably lie on your back in bed and imagine a small room that contains a large cabinet with lots of small drawers.

2. In your mind's eye, take all your worries and enter the room.

3. Now take your worries, and, one at a time, place each in a drawer and close the drawer.

4. Label the outside of the drawer with a word or phrase that captures the essence of that worry.

5. When all the worries are safely tucked away in their drawers, say "good night," turn the light off, and quietly close the door.

6. Now, back in your bed, get in your favorite sleeping position and fall asleep with the knowledge that your worries are resting safely and securely where they belong for the night.

7. If, for some reason, one of the worries gets out of its drawer and wakes you, be sympathetic yet firm in insisting that it climb back into its drawer for the evening. It can wait until morning, after you've had a restful night's sleep.

In any divorce, there is an overriding sense of family sadness. But staying conscious of this sadness makes it sometimes possible to relieve it. Without consciousness, this sadness is transformed into guilt. Or, as one student said about her experience of growing up in a painfully and unconsciously divorced family: "One day I'm going to write a book about the experience, the title of which will be *Guilt*."

Endnotes

1. For an in-depth description of this process I recommend the recent novel by Roddy Doyle, *Paddy Clarke Ha Ha Ha*.

2. A San Francisco non-profit organization, "Kid's Turn," does an excellent job in educating families on the divorce process as well as how to deal with the associated emotions. Kids cope much better with divorce when they understand its terminology and landscape. For more information, write to Kid's Turn, Box 192242, San Francisco, CA 94119, or call (415) 512-4760.

❧ CHAPTER 18 ❧

Remarriage and Blended Families

What is a parent's remarriage like for teenagers?
Is there anything I can do to ease the transition?

There is actually quite a bit that parents can do to ease the process of forming a new family, but you should not gauge the success of the transition by its immediate results—these transitions are usually somewhat awkward, reserved, tense, and messy, no matter how much you intend otherwise. The results of a successful transition are, however, evident down the road. Time and thought invested on the front end of this transition are well-rewarded over the life of the new family.

Remarriage is a confusing concept for adolescents, as it is fraught with built-in conflicts and joys. Let's look at the "simplest" remarriage as an example: a teenage boy's mother is marrying a man who does not have children. On the one hand, the son is pleased that his mother has found someone who makes her content. Yet because it also impacts him as a member of this new family, he must thoroughly address his feelings for his stepfather, which does not occur in a conscious and systematic manner: "Is this someone I could grow to like? Will he try to take over the role of my father? Will he try to push me out of my mother's life? Does he like me? Can I avoid him for the next three years? Do I respect him?" Further, these questions are not asked or answered in a vacuum. The duration of the relationship, the kinds of time the new spouse and adolescent have spent together, preceding relationships, and the environment in which the first marriage ended (death, drawn-out illness, amicable divorce, hostile divorce, affair, etc.) all play vital roles in determining how your teenager responds to the new spouse. Also, your teenager's intellectual abilities can easily mislead you: judge his state of acceptance and readiness more by what he does than by what he says.

In a blended family, the location of the other biological parent and the adolescent's relationship to that parent are crucial factors.

> My mom died when I was in fifth grade, which was pretty awful. My dad met Valerie when I was in eighth grade and they got married last year [tenth grade]. I knew her for a few years before she moved in with us. I was really looking forward to them getting married, so I was a little surprised at how awkward it was at first. I hadn't realized how my dad and I had developed so many routines to keep the house going. Now all of a sudden Valerie was living there too, and of course things were bound to change. At first it was little things, like rearranging the furniture and buying new dishes, which was fine. But when she tore up Mom's garden to redesign the backyard, I went ballistic! I know it was unfair of me to react that way, but it was just too much for me to handle. Obviously, we all got through it, I think in part because I knew Valerie so well beforehand and I wasn't afraid to tell her what I thought. Still, I would recommend other families to start your new family in a different house or apartment; that way everyone begins on more or less even ground with each other.

Living space (with either the addition of the new person into the current space or a move to another space, possibly even to a new school district), living patterns, and family economics all contribute to make remarriage a complex process with many pushes and pulls on both teenagers and adults. Remember, it isn't the adolescent who is initiating the new family. Adolescents must react (see especially Chapters 2 and 3), so it is best to find ways for them to be as active as possible in the development of new family norms and logistics. They don't want or need to be a full partner in this process, as their lives are quite busy already, but they do need to be consulted regularly for input.

When my mom married Jack she really wanted me to feel included. In fact, she dragged me to every open house in the area before I finally had to call a stop to it. I mean who has the time or energy to spend every Sunday going in and out of other people's houses? So I just told her what I wanted: to stay in the same school district, to have my own room, and to have a chance to see the place before they bought it. From then on everything was fine.

From the teenager's perspective, remarriage implies "taking the place of" and "forgetting," which can cause anger. If not consciously discussed, these thoughts fuel all the negatives of remarriage. In divorced families this happens when the new spouse tries to be or is perceived as trying to be a parent, and in widowed families when the deceased spouse is not discussed from time to time within the new family. When either of these happen, the adolescent is in the unenviable position of having to loyally hold onto the family history. To "forget" or "replace" a parent is a frightening proposition to teenagers. It is best if he is encouraged to remember the other parent. Otherwise, a part of him is lost, as well as fueling the often but not always unconscious fear that he too can be "forgotten" or "replaced." In the following story, the son's parents had divorced five years earlier and the father had moved out of the area, only seeing his son during the summer.

I couldn't believe what happened when my mom got remarried. Bill had been OK until then. But all of a sudden he was trying to be my father: telling me what to do, when to study, when to go to bed, and even coming to my games and cheering me on like I was his son! When we moved into his house, he insisted that I leave my old furniture behind because he had already picked out new stuff for me, stuff that went with the house. Hell, I liked my old bed just fine! Also, before getting married he used to ask me about my father and the kinds of things we did when I was a kid and over the summer. But afterward he didn't want to hear about it. In fact, when my mom and I would mention something from the past, he would act like a hurt puppy, usually just walking away. Of course my mom would hurry after him to make everything OK. He even tried to get me to skip a summer with my dad so we could all go away together!

In the above story, the new spouse is clearly both too eager and too sensitive. Stepparents need patience and thick skins. A relationship with a teenager takes time to develop. Let things happen as naturally as possible. Also, as difficult as it is, let and even invite teenagers to talk about their childhoods and the parent who is not there. This kind of talk isn't a slander against you; rather it is how adolescents integrate their histories with the present. Let them gracefully hold onto their histories.

Now, rather than going through all the possible permutations of newly formed families, let's look at a few issues that are constants: siblings, parental roles, and living space.

Biological siblings are a natural source of support and constancy for one another in any change to the family structure. In various custody arrangements, it is usually in everyone's best interest to keep the kids together in their movements between households. Especially in cases of joint custody, kids with siblings have a stronger sense of stability and support. In cases where two parents with kids get together and make a new family, there are a host of complications to consider. The parents may be in love but the kids are not. They will need time to develop their own relationships with one another, and it won't happen overnight. While you are hoping for deep friendships between them, it is an unrealistic expectation. Perhaps respectful tolerance is all one can honestly hope for. Let it happen naturally; if you push your expectations, you will probably get the opposite of what you want. The kids must have their say in this.

When a new family is formed through remarriage, the spouses must be clear on their parental roles with the kids. With teenagers it is best if the biological parent assumes most of the direct parenting responsibilities, especially in the areas of structure and the enforcement of natural consequences. It is unfair to expect a stepparent to play that role; it hardly ever works and it creates undue and inevitable resentment between the adolescent and the new spouse.

When Cherie and my dad got married I think she was pretty confused about how to treat me. It was especially odd because when my parents were still married it was my mom who did most of the discipline and stuff like that. I think my dad must have subconsciously expected Cherie to do the same. But after one or two attempts at that, she and I both knew that it would never work, so she backed off quite a bit. Then for awhile it was like nobody was watching me, and I went a bit overboard. It was hard for awhile, but it got better when my father finally began acting like my father. Now I'm a freshman in college and Cherie and I are pretty good friends. I like talking to her when I call home, and sometimes I even prefer talking to her!

The non-biological parent has a tough line to walk, and it's different with each child, depending on personality and age. What works with a seven-year-old probably won't be effective with a seventeen-year-old. In many respects the non-biological parent is like an aunt or uncle to the adolescent. But no matter what, it is essential that they form their own relationship based on their personalities. Don't rest on the assumption that a working relationship will happen. What is most important is that the teenager and new spouse come to genuinely respect one another, and this is something that is earned over time. Also, if the new spouse is not interested in forming a relationship with the adolescent, it is unfair to go ahead; try waiting on the marriage until the adolescent is out of the house. A lack of interest is perceived by teenagers as overwhelming rejection.

My mom's husband seems like a nice guy, but we don't have any sort of relationship. If we're all together and my mom walks out of the room, we have nothing to say to each other and usually pick up books or turn on the TV. I'm not sure why; I guess he just doesn't like me. I've tried to get to know him. I've asked about work, about his family, and even about sports, but I never get more than a one-sentence response, like I'm bothering him or something. I can't wait to get out of this house.

Clearly, in considering remarriage, it is grossly irresponsible to ignore the impact it will have on the kids. And it's naive to believe that it can succeed if your new spouse does not have some sort of working relationship with them.

Space is another important concept when a new family is formed. This is especially true when both spouses bring kids to the new family. Whether the custody arrangement is full- or half-time, it is essential that your adolescent have a space of her own—whether it is her own room or at least secure storage for her things. And let her (within the structure of your home) do with it what she wants. But most of all, ensure that it is a private and safe place for her. This is a retreat for her within her own home, much like the after-school story in Chapter 3. Expect it to be more so within the blended family.

> Both my parents have remarried people with kids, so it is all pretty confusing. The only sane part is that I have my own room in each house that I've gotten to decorate exactly how I want. And nobody goes in the room when I'm not there. (At my father's house there is even a lock on the door because his wife has nosey little kids!) Whenever I come back to one of the houses, my room is exactly how I left it, which somehow gives me some security.

All in all, it takes a few years for a blended family to solidify; it doesn't happen overnight, which is why it is important not to evaluate the new family too soon. After the first few blowups or shouting matches, it is easy to doubt the potential for long-term success, but this is premature. Often the most difficult and the most important consideration in the creation of a new family is your expectations. You must be realistic. If you cling to an idealized fantasy of how the new family should be, it will be a miserable experience for everyone involved. Always remain willing to reevaluate your expectations.

Adolescence is a turbulent time in and of itself, so when the structure changes significantly, the turbulence increases—but so does the need for consistency. The only means for the adolescent to gain security about all this is to frequently test the limits, especially in the first couple of years. As always, be persistently patient.

❧ CHAPTER 19 ❧

Single Parenting

What are the unique difficulties in single parenting, and what is the best way to deal with them?

Single parenting is not tremendously different from parenting with a spouse—just exponentially more difficult and complex. First, the single parent is continually "on" with their teenager. They can never simply turn to their partner, have them instantly understand, and retire to the bedroom for some rest and solitude while the crisis is addressed. The buck always stops in the same place. Being "on" requires lots of energy and attention, which a parent does not always have, and one is prone to more mistakes.

> Even though my husband passed away seven years ago, I still catch myself thinking, "Go ask your father" when John interrupts me with an urgent request or question. It is such a pain to stop what I'm doing in order to give John my full attention, but whenever I give him less than full attention I pay for it in the long run. For instance, a couple of weeks ago he came into the study on a Thursday night while I was working. He wanted to know if it was OK to go out to a party with Josh on Friday night and stay out an hour past curfew. He needed to know right then because Josh was waiting on the phone. By his voice I could tell that there was something else hidden in the question, but I brushed it aside and let it pass, returning to my work after quickly giving my permission. Well, it was the next night when my inattentive attitude came back to haunt me. John "forgot"

to tell me that Josh was driving (on his four-day old license!), and that the party was in the next town! Of course all this came to my attention twenty minutes before he was getting picked up. Needless to say we had a very messy scene, and when it was over I vowed (for about the hundredth time), to pay 100 percent attention to John's requests and hidden agendas, and most of all, to trust that parental voice in me that smells a rat.

Along with the pressure of always being "on," the single parent is also without the benefit of reflective conversation. Even after a couple has blown it in some way with their teenager, they still have the option to huddle with one another to learn from their mistakes, plan for the future, rethink strategies and approaches, and above all, support one another. The single parent does not have this shared, reflective experience. They have the solitude of their own thoughts, which, as we have seen elsewhere, tend to focus on mistakes. Without this reflective dialogue they have less of a chance of breaking out of or creatively understanding the cycle they're in with their kids. Finding other single parents to spend time with and to talk to about various parent-adolescent concerns is immensely helpful, in fact, essential. But often, you must actively invite others into these conversations.

Sarah's father left when she was in the first grade; since then it has been just her and me. Grammar school and middle school were fairly smooth, though the second half of eighth grade was tough. At one of her soccer games early in the fall, I introduced myself to a few of the other kids' moms and dads. It turned out that two of them were also single parents. Later that fall, as Sarah seemed to be changing faster than I could keep track of, I invited those two parents over for dinner. I wanted to find out if similar things were happening in their homes: Reggie's daughter was a sophomore and Ceila's daughter was a freshman. After some initial awkwardness we started to talk fairly honestly about our relations with our kids. In a weird way it was refreshing to hear that they were encountering many of the same difficulties that I was. It was also useful to hear how they understood and addressed the various problems. By the evening's end I felt like my "bag of tricks" had been replenished. It was a great night! We all felt more hopeful and optimistic about our kids and ourselves. Since then we've met for dinner every few months. It's strange; none of us is friends outside of these dinners, yet I count them as very important people in my life.

As a single parent you may have plenty of friends and an active social life, yet at the same time spend little time with anyone who understands and appreciates the toll that single parenting takes on you. If you don't have access to other single parents for one reason or another, think seriously about seeing a local psychologist or family therapist for periodic consultations about parenting. Granted, this is a different arrangement and purpose than in most therapeutic relationships, but nonetheless one that many professionals are comfortable with—just be clear about what you want up front.

Obviously, single parenting requires a major sacrifice of personal time. From a simple logistics perspective, you are doing the job of two people by yourself. With time you can teach your teenager to assume more and more responsibility, but no matter how good they are, the ultimate authority always rests with you. With this increased responsibility comes a subtle trap: you invest too much of your personal esteem and identity into your adolescent's life. She becomes an extension of you which, over the long run, leaves you uncomfortably vulnerable to her performance (in academics, sports, social life, drama, dance, the arts). Over time, this is a particularly seductive trap, because initially (prior to and during the initial stages of adolescence), it is so successful and rewarding.

> You sacrifice personal time for your daughter. She is openly grateful. You miss out on personal opportunities because you are a good parent. She openly flourishes as she grows with your added attention. You want more and more for her, mostly for her overall well-being and in part as a means to justify your sacrifices. She works hard, because she wants

the same things for herself that you want for her. The two of you are following essentially the same blueprint. Her successes motivate you to sacrifice more; you begin to take and enjoy her successes personally. She continues to work hard, wanting to make you proud. Then she hits adolescence. You continue to bask in her various successes, but you also begin to take her inevitable "failures" personally. And worst of all, she is no longer open to your input. In fact, she is quite confused. You respond by directing her more precisely—you attempt to do a "better job." She resists. You insist. She rebels. You yell. And it all escalates quite quickly—in fact, more quickly and powerfully each time.

This is not a healthy pattern for either the adult or the teenager. (Single parents should read carefully Chapter 20, as it applies doubly to them, and is the best antidote to this pattern.)

Finally, as if all the preceding isn't enough, you're faced with increased economic pressure that not only affects your relationship with your adolescent, but also affects how you evaluate yourself as a parent.

The worst is right before I go to sleep after we've had an argument. Not only do I play the fight over in my head about a hundred times—usually focusing on his faults in the first fifty versions and mine in the second fifty—but then I move beyond the fight to include most of my other inadequacies as a parent. In that script, finances are a biggie! Somehow I feel like money should be a secure given. I mean, my parents couldn't have worried this much about paying bills, financing college, fixing the plumbing, and attempting to have a credible career, could they? Anyway, I do a real number on myself in this area. It basically comes down to this: If we have any economic crisis I feel like a failure as a person and as an adult—I know, not too logical, but nonetheless...

From the teenager's perspective, having only one active parent means a 50 percent loss of parental diversity in their life, and the effects of this loss are far-reaching. Without another parent, it is easier for the adolescent to get locked into one role with their remaining parent.

> One of us always seems to be in Charissa's good graces while the other is the bad guy, though over time it seems to balance out. If one of us has been the bad guy for a long time, we make sure to switch roles. If my wife has been the bad guy, we'll make sure that I do the "reminding" about chores and the denying of extended curfew, while my wife gives her movie money and compliments her on her piano playing. This way she always feels safe with one of us should she need to confide in us.

Without two parents, the adolescent also loses the modeling of how two adults who love one another successfully fight: how they can disagree, argue, yell, and finally reach a successful resolution. Nor does the teenager experience how they can influence one parent about their perspective and see the other acquiesce in trust to the other parent and adolescent. Leaps of parental faith are more common with two parents than with one. Finally, with one parent, there is obviously only one gender present for the teenager to observe.

The solution to this is simple: Get more adults involved in your adolescent's life. Teachers and coaches can play a vital role. Encourage your son to get close to a teacher, or encourage a coach to take a more active role in your daughter's life (see Chapter 12). Look into summer experiences that place your son in proximity to caring adults: camps, youth programs, church organizations. The difficult part of this is to not get jealous when the strategy begins to work.

> At first it was great when William got close to Phil (the camp director at the local Y.M.C.A.) when he worked as a counselor at the day camp. But after a while I got tired of hearing "Phil" stories. Then I even began to get jealous.

This guy was telling William the same things I had been telling him for fifteen years, yet this guy was a demigod and I was plain old mom! Ah well, such is parenthood.

In any single-parent family, the teenager inevitably assumes more responsibility than she would otherwise. This is not necessarily good or bad, but it does happen (see Chapter 17 for more on adolescents' increased responsibilities). While most teenagers cannot acknowledge it during their adolescence, they are aware of all that you do for them (and do not do for yourself.) It just takes time for that feedback to come around.

Dad

It's the man with the whistle
who made us spaghetti,
covered with hot dog bits.
He taught us life and basketball,
play for the team, box out,
but no foul outs. Bought us bikes,
mini-bikes, and snowmobiles to crash.
For years I've been witness to the chameleon golf swing,
back and forth across the grass
never reaching the green.

He drove me to St. Louis
All of us went to the Arch
and stayed far from the airport.
He has given me material
which he impressed as trivial,
none have lasted like the lessons
he has taught us: compassion,
simple fun and a Family
grown from his saintly heart.
Somebody should call Hallmark
and create a new card day
for fathers who are moms.

Tim Riera

❧ CHAPTER 20 ❦

Parent Mental Health

*With all that is happening with our kids,
what can we do to take care of ourselves
during the tumultuous years of adolescence?*

Taking care of your mental health is one of the best examples you can set for your kids. As noted earlier, by adolescence your kids are learning more by what you do than by what you say, as hard as that is to take. Without conscious attention, your spousal relationship, your continued intellectual and emotional growth, and your personal pursuits will all take resentful back seats to the trauma of adolescence. It is important to make and take time for these aspects of your life without abandoning your teenager. These aspects must be built into the fabric of your life. It's like saving money. You know the story: Unsuccessful savers typically pay their bills, spend the grocery money, allocate a certain amount of spending money, set aside some for unexpected expenses, and deposit the remaining two dollars in their savings account. Successful savers follow a completely different recipe. They pick an amount they are going to save every month and pay their savings account first. Then they deal with the rest. The same is true with your mental health: Pay yourself first.

Ideally, you do something to feed your mental health on a daily basis, no matter for how short a time. My t'ai chi instructor, Lenzie Williams, calls this minimum and maximum practice routines. In studying t'ai chi, an ideal goal might be one hour of practice a day, which would be ambitious. Typically one would do quite well with this goal for, say about five days—at which point you would miss a day, then practice well a couple of more days before missing another day. Needless to say, after a few weeks you would be missing more days than you are practicing. And after a few more weeks you would probably give up on t'ai chi and move onto something else entirely. But now you have a guilt hangover. However, with minimum and maximum practice routines you can have the goal of ten minutes a day as a minimum practice and, say, one hour a day as a maximum practice, with anything in between ten minutes and one hour satisfactory (or at least guilt-free). Chances are that if you practiced in this manner for the same four weeks you would have practiced more overall, and most important, still be interested in the activity. And, of course, you would have no guilt hangover. In fact, you would be feeling quite good about yourself. The same is true with your mental health and parenting. Do at least a minimal amount of whatever nurtures your mental health on a daily basis.

> I love to read. So every day I make sure I read at least a couple of pages of whatever novel I'm into at the time. Sometimes I get my pages in on the bus or at the laundromat, but no matter what, I always get a few in every day. And it really makes a difference. When I get a stretch of an hour or so, I can really get lost in whatever I'm reading. Maybe it's an escape, but I prefer to see it as time purely for me, which, given everything else I do, seems more than fair.

And,

> There's actually no one thing I do daily, but every day I consciously do something for myself, no matter how small. For instance, when I have the time I work in the garden, or go for a jog, or go out for coffee with a friend, or smoke a cigar on the back porch. And when I'm short for time I still manage something—maybe a walk down the street, or two minutes of listening to a favorite song; or maybe I'll just massage my feet for a couple of minutes before going to sleep.

For parental mental health, the mantra is: "Don't take it personally." Remember, your teenager is in a phase different from all previous stages of development. Prior to this stage most parents are quite willing, and even eager, to take their child's behavior personally. They bask in the joy and accomplishments of their kids through childhood, so the "don't take it personally" stance of adolescence is perplexing.

> I remember watching a close friend's five-year-old daughter crawl onto his lap, wrap her arms around him, take a deep sigh, and say, "Daddy, I love you. You're the smartest and nicest daddy in the world!" His heart practically came out of his chest! And I heard a little voice in the back of my head say, "Enjoy it now, but don't hold it against her when she is sixteen and doesn't think nearly so highly of you."

Teenagers can be quite critical of their parents—sometimes justifiably, but often not. With all that is going on with them (see Chapter 2) they are usually just venting their frustration in a place they feel is safe. Very few teenagers, after an evening of arguing with their parents, come home to find the locks changed and a sign hanging on the door: "We're tired of your constant arguing. Go away and come back when you've grown up. Love, Mom and Dad." So in a twisted sort of way, their venting on you is a compliment. While adolescents aren't pleased with the arguing, it is the only "safe place" for them to sort through and make sense of their changing lives. It is also why clear structures and limits are crucial.

For your ongoing mental health as a parent, it is important to break down the isolation of adolescent parenting by making friends with the parents of other teenagers. Talk with other parents about what is really happening in your home, both the good and the bad. If you just focus on the good (and keep the negative silently to yourself) you'll walk away worse than ever, convinced that you really are an atrocious parent. If you only talk about the bad, you'll walk away depressed and hopeless, which isn't much better. By discussing the good and the bad, you will realize that what is happening in your home isn't all that different than what is happening in other adolescent homes. This in itself makes it easier to not take things so personally. (For additional ideas on this topic, see Chapter 19.)

Finally, remember that a large part of your role as parent is to nurture your teenager's hope. At the same time, remember to take care of your own hope too. It is what will keep you going, even on the toughest of days.

CHAPTER 21

Professional Help

What are the signs that professional help is needed, and how do I go about getting it?

How to decide when help is appropriate is often a more difficult matter than actually getting the assistance. Of course, this task is obvious if your teenager approaches you with a request for help (and sometimes it happens that way), but more often than not it is you deciding that they (or both of you) need some assistance, with them initially resisting the idea stubbornly.

> Whenever I mention the idea of seeing a therapist about the divorce, Thomas [adolescent son] just glares at me and walks away. Therapy has been essential for me, so I want him to get the same kind of benefit, but he absolutely refuses.

Basically, professional help is indicated whenever you feel that health and safety are in jeopardy and you feel powerless to positively affect the situation. It is one thing for your teenager to get poor grades, but an entirely different matter to repeatedly come home drunk. The difficulty here is in allowing yourself to accurately assess the severity of the situation; once an honest assessment is made, the question of professional help is the next step.

> In retrospect I can see that Shelly was in trouble for quite a while, it was just that we refused to recognize or believe it. She had lost a great deal of weight, wasn't going out with friends anymore, never ate in front of us, and exercised

obsessively. But it didn't all click until one of her teachers called us, deeply concerned about her health. I can't believe we didn't see it ourselves, but obviously we didn't.

Accurately assessing the situation is the most difficult part. Parents, because they want to believe the best about their kids, are in a difficult position to fully recognize what is going on. Because of this, other parents can be a great resource. Also, feel free to call teachers and coaches just to check in about how your teenager is doing. (Don't ask them directly about the problem, since few are in the position to answer directly and with accuracy. Also, asking this undermines adolescents and the world they are developing away from home.) Serious problems seldom limit themselves to one aspect of a person's life.

We were concerned about Byron's late-night activities, as we had found beer caps in the car on several occasions. Of course, he told us they were isolated incidents, and we were more than willing to believe him. But after the third incident I decided to call a few of his teachers, along with his baseball coach, just to get a general impression of how he was doing in their eyes. It turned out that of the four adults I called, two were very worried about him and another expressed concern. We clearly had to look at the situation much more closely, this time without our parent-blinders on.

Basically, there are three entrance points into assessing a problem area. The first focuses on education and discussion before a problem arises. This typically occurs at home and school. For example, a speaker comes into a health class to talk about alcohol and drug abuse. The students receive lots of information about the topic, hear a personal account, and have an opportunity for questions, discussion, and reflection.

The second entrance point occurs after a problem has been recognized but is still not debilitating to the person. Again this happens at home and school, but is often augmented with professional assistance. An example is the mother who catches her teenager drinking or under the influence of marijuana. Something is definitely amiss, but it still might not be disabling. This situation requires honest discussion, a re-examination of family guidelines and agreements, information on drugs and alcohol (for both parents and adolescent), and possibly the services of a counselor.

The final entrance point occurs after the problem is established and turned into a disability. This requires professional assistance and may, in extreme instances, include some sort of residential treatment. An example is the teenager who is so depressed that he doesn't have the energy to get out of bed for weeks at a time. At the minimum, this requires direct and ongoing professional intervention.

Once you make the decision that professional help is in order, be firm and insistent. Give your adolescent a choice in choosing who to see and under what circumstances, but not a choice over whether you seek assistance. If he obstinately refuses to see a professional of your choice, they [the professionals] usually have a variety of means of getting the adolescent to come in, or of working indirectly through you. I know of a counselor who met with an entire family minus the adolescent and simply sent the adolescent a summary letter of every meeting. Eventually the adolescent insisted upon coming in, since the letters reflected a great deal of inaccuracies around her behavior, at least in her mind. Also, there are times when you might seek a professional consultation for yourself about parenting issues (see Chapter 19).

When you have determined that your teenager and you need professional assistance, there are several points to keep in mind. First and foremost is that you have a great deal of choice. When you are meeting with professionals (whether they are psychologists, psychiatrists, family therapists, nutritionists, tutors, or gynecologists) remember that you are the consumer. Treat first meetings as part of the shopping-around phase. Beyond the education and skills of this person, you are looking for someone you can trust and respect. Give your teenager the same freedom.

Second, in your shopping-around period, ask the professionals any and all questions you have—don't worry about being rude. How much do they charge? Who do they meet with—the adolescent alone, parents alone, everyone together? How confidential is what you say? What your adolescent says?

Third, the best source for the names of helpful professionals are your friends, specifically the friends who also are parents of adolescents. Most parents of adolescents have either made use of or know of somebody who has summoned professional help. Don't be shy about asking; it doesn't mean you're a failure as a parent. Also, make use of the personnel at your school; deans, vice-principals, and counselors will all have potential referrals. After securing their confidentiality, make sure to give them enough information so they can be helpful, especially in determining the type of professional assistance you require.

> When I realized what was happening with Celia I didn't know where to turn. For lack of a better starting point, I called her guidance counselor, who directed me to the school counselor. She was very helpful in describing the various types of professional help available and suitable for what was happening with Celia. On top of that, she gave me several names to call and the titles of a couple of books to read. She was very helpful.

❦ CHAPTER 22 ❦

Concluding Remarks

This book has probably stirred memories for you—of your own youth and your own past and future as a parent. The adage "what goes around comes around" is in many ways the cornerstone of the parent-adolescent relationship. Inevitably, aspects of the relationship are messy—just like good education. Thus, parents needn't expect themselves to get it right the first time through. In fact, you'll probably blow it at least as much as you succeed, like any decent therapist, who constantly needs "correcting" by the client. Trust me, you'll have another chance; it'll always come around again. This book is very much for the reflective parent—something to refer to after you've blown it and need to think it through again in order to improve your earlier performance.

If nothing else, I hope this book has conveyed the fact there are no tried-and-true prescriptions for successfully parenting teenagers. There are, however, attitudes and understandings that are crucial. Personally, I believe the horizons described in Chapter 2 are quite useful in understanding most adolescent behaviors, and for appreciating the context of the adolescent years. And during adolescence, context is just about everything. The horizons also allow you to stay involved, creative, and curious with your teenager, so that you will try different approaches and behaviors with your child rather than trying the same things over and over with fewer and fewer successes.

It is useful to remember that, like it or not, you are much more of a consultant than a manager for your teenager (except when it comes to health and safety issues). Thinking in terms of influence is much more useful and sane than thinking in terms of control.

Parenting adolescents is uniquely difficult because they are alternately (and sometimes simultaneously) in two different stages of life: childhood and adulthood. Your job is to provide the environment that lets them grow into adulthood in a healthy manner rather than regress back to childhood in unhealthy ways. After all, adolescence is about passion and about learning how to use that passion in constructive and conscious ways. Probably the best you can do here is to maintain consistency, love, hope, and a deep faith that they'll get through it all successfully. In short, love them for what they are, not for what they have the potential of becoming.

But it is also clear that parenting is an art. And like any art, it is limitless in its possibilities. Also, like any art, the more proficient you become at parenting the more room you see for improvement. At the same time, then, parenting is a craft, something you can always learn to do better.

Finally, I offer the words of Robert Pirsig, author of *Zen and the Art of Motorcycle Maintenance*, on, of all things, the instructions for putting together a rotisserie.

> These rotisserie instructions [read parenting instructions] begin and end exclusively with the machine [read the adolescent]. But the kind of approach I'm thinking about doesn't cut it off so narrowly. What's really angering about instructions of this sort is that they imply there's only one way to put this rotisserie together—their way. And that presumption wipes out all the creativity. Actually there are hundreds of ways to put the rotisserie together and when they make you follow just one way without showing you the overall problem, the instructions become hard to follow in such a way as not to make mistakes. You lose feeling for the work. And not only that, it's very unlikely that they've told you the best way.... And when you presume there's just one right way to do things, of course the instructions begin and end exclusively with the rotisserie. But if you have to choose among an infinite number of ways to put it together, then the relation of the machine to you, and the relation of the

machine and you to the rest of the world, has to be considered, because the selection from among many choices, the art of the work is just as dependent upon your own mind and spirit as it is upon the material of the machine. That's why you need the peace of mind.

Carl Jung offers a slightly different perspective: "Consciousness is not achieved without pain." From this viewpoint, raising a teenager provides numerous opportunities for leaps of consciousness. And this is difficult (but worth remembering) when your teenager's room is empty at 2:00 a.m., when the phone isn't ringing, when the vice principal is asking for a meeting, when you are buying a gown for the prom, when you are *not* buying a gown for the prom, after you have found an empty beer can in the car. When all is said and done, they need and want you as allies, not enemies, during this confusing and vital phase of life.

❧ BIBLIOGRAPHY ❧

Bruner, Jerome. *Actual Minds, Possible Worlds*. Cambridge: Harvard University Press, 1986.

Coburn, Karen and Madge Treeger. *Letting Go: A Parent's Guide to Today's College Experience*. Bethesda: Adler and Adler, 1992.

Doyle, Roddy. *Paddy Clarke Ha Ha Ha*. New York: Viking, 1993.

Dreikurs, Rudolf. *Children: The Challenge*. New York: Hawthorn/Dutton, 1964.

Elium, Jeanne and Don. *Raising a Daughter*. Berkeley: Celestial Arts, 1994.

Fairchild & Hayward. *Now That You Know: What Every Parent Should Know About Homosexuality*. San Diego: Harcourt Brace Jovanovich, 1979.

Furman, Ben and Tapani Ahola. *Solution Talk: Hosting Therapeutic Conversations*. New York: W. W. Norton, 1992.

Gilligan, Carol. *In a Different Voice*. Cambridge: Harvard University Press, 1982.

Greenberg-Lake: The Analysis Group, Inc. *"Shortchanging Girls, Shortchanging America."* Washington, D.C.: American Association of University Women, 1991.

Grollman, Earl A. *Straight Talk about Death for Teenagers*. Boston: Beacon Press, 1993.

Heron, Ann. *One Teenager in Ten: Writings by Gay and Lesbian Youth*. Boston: Alyson Publications, 1983.

Inaba, Darryl S. and William E. Cohen. *Uppers, Downers, and All Arounders*. Ashland, Oregon: CNS Productions, 1993.

Kinsey, Alfred and others. *Sexual Behavior in the Human Female*. Philadelphia: W.B. Saunders, 1953.

Kinsey, Pomeroy, and Martin. S*exual Behavior in the Human Male*. Philadelphia: W.B. Saunders, 1948.

Kübler-Ross, Elizabeth. *On Death and Dying*. New Haven: Yale University Press, 1968.

Laumann, Edward O. and others. *The Social Organization of Sexuality*. Chicago: University of Chicago Press, 1993.

Lidz, Theodore. *The Person: His Development throughout the Life Cycle*. New York: Basic Books, 1968.

Mayher, William S. "The Dynamics of Senior Year: A Report from the Frontlines." Tarrytown, New York: Hackly School, 1989.

McNaught, Brian. *On Being Gay: Thoughts on Family, Faith, and Love*. New York: St. Martin's Press, 1988.

Pirsig, Robert. *Zen and the Art of Motorcycle Maintenance*. New York: Quill William Morrow, 1974.

Riera, Michael. "A Phenomenological Analysis of Best-Friendship in Preadolescent Boys," Ph.D. diss., California Institute of Integral Studies, San Francisco, 1992.

Shedler, Jonathan and Jack Block. "Adolescent Drug Use and Psychological Health: A Longitudinal Inquiry." *American Psychologist*, May 1990.

Stewart, D.L. "On Being a Dad: A Teen's Lesson in Lurching." *San Francisco Chronicle*, San Francisco, 21 August 1991.

White, Michael and David Epston. *Literate Means to Therapeutic Ends*. Adelaide, Australia: Dulwich Centre Publications, 1989.

❊ INDEX ❊

A

Abstract thinking, 13-14
  friendships and, 42
Academics. *see also* Homework
  in eleventh grade, 47
  grades, 107-115
  motivation, encouragement of,
    112-115
  in ninth grade, 40-41
  questions about, 108-109
  in twelfth grade, 56
Acting out, 28
Addiction, theory of, 99-100
Advice-giving, 147-149
Advisor role of parents. *See*
  Consultant-parent
Ahola, Tapani, 35, 85
AIDS, 121
  sex education and, 123
Alcohol, 93-106. *see also* Drugs
  description of, 99
  driving and drinking, 156-157
  grieving and use of, 175
  loneliness and use of, 150
  lying about, 88
  professional help for abuse,
    208-209
  social issues of using, 94-95
Amphetamines (speed), 98
Anorexia. *See* Eating disorders
Athletics, 41, 141-145
Autonomy, 53

B

Behavior norms, 14
Birth control, 121, 124

Blame, 26
  reciprocal blaming, 85
Blended families, 191-196
Block, Jack, 96-97
Bodybuilding, 166
Breaking up, 119-121
Bribery for grades, 113
Brothers and sisters. *See* Siblings
Bruner, Jerome, 36
Bulimia. *See* Eating disorders

C

Cameras at college, 66
Cannabis, 98
Car privileges, 81
  designated drivers, 105-106
  drinking and driving, 156-157
  driver's license, 48, 153-160
  natural consequences and, 84
  as power issue, 155
  responsibility and, 155-156
Center for Population Options, 122
Ciardi, John, 35
Clothes, 23
Cocaine, 98
Cognitive maturity, 11-15
College
  junior year and, 47-48
  non-college bound students,
    55-56
  over-parenting and, 76-77
  parents and, 54-55
  separation at, 65
  stress and, 53-54
  twelfth grade year and, 53-54
Commencement message, 66-71
Common questions, viii-ix